Elegant Bride's

1000 Questions About
Your Wedding

Elegant Bride's
1000 Questions About Your Wedding

by Jaclyn C. Barrett-Hirschhaut

THE SUMMIT PUBLISHING GROUP
Arlington, Texas

◪ THE SUMMIT PUBLISHING GROUP
One Arlington Centre, 1112 East Copeland Road, Fifth Floor
Arlington, Texas 76011
summit@dfw.net
www.summitbooks.com

Printed in the United States of America.

01 00 99 98 97   5 4 3 2 1

Library of Congress Cataloging-in-Publication Data

Barrett-Hirschhaut, Jaclyn C. (Jaclyn Celia), 1954-
    Elegant bride's 1000 questions about your wedding / by
        Jaclyn C. Barrett-Hirschhaut.
        Includes index.
    ISBN 1-56530-266-4 (pbk.)
        1. Weddings—United States—Planning.   I. Title. II. Title:
        Elegant bride's one thousand questions about your
        wedding.
HQ745.B376 1997
395.2'2'0973—dc21   97-33878
                                                          CIP

Cover design by Dennis Davidson
Book design by Michael Melton
Cover photograph by Scott Crowder
Black-and-white photography by Robert Isacson
Index by Joyce Kay Goldenstein

To Bruce and Eric, the Hirschhaut men who are the
light of my life.

To Pat and John Gammerino, who taught me to think for
myself and who inspired me to follow my dreams.

To all of my colleagues at *Elegant Bride*, who continually strive
to create the preeminent wedding periodical
dedicated to elegance, tradition, and grand style
that is an invaluable source of information and advice
for so many women.

To Robert Isacson, of Blackmore & Isacson in Potomac,
Maryland, whose outstanding photography
evokes beautiful imagery of wonderful wedding celebrations.

Contents

Introduction   ix

1 Your Engagement   1

2 Beginning to Plan   29

3 The Bridal Party   51

4 Wedding Fashions   69

5 Wedding Jewelry/Accessories   117

6 Invitations/Stationery   137

7 Flowers   191

8 Music   231

9 Photography/Videography   259

10 Bridal Gift Registry   289

11 The Marriage Ceremony   327

12 The Wedding Reception   363

13 Cakes   401

14 The Honeymoon   419

15 Your First Home   441

Introduction

HE POPS THE QUESTION...AND SHE ANSWERS "YES." NOW there are hundreds of decisions—his church or hers, what kind of dress and formalwear to choose, where to register for gifts. A simple wedding band or a ring of diamonds? Mixed drinks or lots of champagne? An island honeymoon or perhaps Paris?

My career as the editor-in-chief of *Elegant Bride* magazine has provided me with substantial professional fulfillment and significant personal gratitude. I have always been appreciative of the opportunity to expand my experience in the fields of journalism, marketing, and retailing by joining this magazine's staff in anticipation of its first anniversary issue. The months and years have passed all too quickly, and today I share tremendous pride in celebrating the tenth anniversary of producing an award-winning publication.

Since *Elegant Bride* has always prided itself on its tasteful, thought-provoking articles and instructive pictures, it seems only natural to create an easy-to-read source for planning the most meaningful of life's occasions—the wedding day. And while everyone knows that there are wedding celebrations of every style, size, and extravagance, I have attempted to provide a complete primer that addresses all of the many details that need to be arranged.

It is my sincere hope that your wedding celebration is a dream come true, with memories that last a lifetime.

1

Your Engagement

∞1∞

Q What tradition prompts today's groom-to-be to formally ask the bride-to-be's father for her hand in marriage?

1

A In the earliest days of the human race, the betrothal ritual involved an exchange of gifts or property from the groom-to-be to the bride-to-be's parents. This was not only ceremonial, but an important part of the marriage contract due to the fact that the bride's family was losing her to another lineage forever, and thus sought compensation, hence the bride's price.

Once a highly negotiated process to establish the terms of the union between a man and a woman, the betrothal eventually gave way in the eighteenth century to a more refined courtship whereby a groom chose his bride for reasons of love.

Following the era of the arranged marriage when the groom would specify the exact payment he offered for his future wife, the formality of a groom asking the bride-to-be's father for her hand in marriage preserves a trace of history and often serves to cement the relationship between the groom-to-be and his future father-in-law.

∞2∞

Q Must the groom present his bride with an engagement ring at the moment of the proposal of marriage?

Although many grooms-to-be take pleasure in slipping an engagement ring on their fiancée's finger along with the offering proposal, it is certainly not a requirement for a couple when pledging their love to each other. In today's modern age, many couples spend time together shopping for the engagement ring either before or after the conversations that lead to the formal proposal.

What are some of the most popular ways for a groom-to-be to propose marriage?

A proposal can be expressed during a quiet time at home, with the groom-to-be getting down on bended knee and presenting a ring. Many grooms-to-be employ a restaurant waiter to share in the process by placing the engagement ring in the bride-to-be's champagne glass, or by delivering a dessert inscribed with the question "Will you marry me?" or having a fortune cookie specially made with the proposal written inside.

What is the origin of the engagement ring?

Engagement, or betrothal, rings date back to the ancient days of marriage by purchase when gold

rings were circulated as currency. The groom-to-be
would offer his bride-to-be a gold ring both as his
partial payment and as a symbol of his intentions.

What are some historical practices of engagement
rings?

Primitive brides-to-be wore woven bands made of rush (a flexible marsh plant with hollow stems), and replaced them each year. Roman brides-to-be wore rings made of iron to symbolize the permanent, unending nature of marriage. During Medieval times, grooms-to-be placed the ring on three of the bride's fingers in turn to represent the Holy Trinity—the Father, the Son, and the Holy Spirit.

Q What is a gimmal ring?

The gimmal ring originated during the Elizabethan period and is a set of three interlocking rings. During the engagement, the bride-to-be, groom-to-be, and their witness each wore one of the rings until the wedding day when the three pieces were united as a single ring for the bride.

Q Who pays for the engagement ring?

It is customary for the groom-to-be to cover the expense of the engagement ring for his bride. Because of the cost of some engagement rings and wedding bands, it is certainly acceptable for the bride-to-be to contribute to the purchase of her ring.

༄8༄

Q Why is the engagement ring placed on the third finger of the left hand?

A In ancient times, this finger was believed to be the only one with a vein running directly to the heart. Therefore, it was believed that a ring on this finger would ensure a long and loving marriage.

༄9༄

Q Why is the diamond the most popular gem in an engagement ring?

A Diamonds are the hardest and most durable of stones with a sparkle said to arise from the flame of love. The symbol of innocence, most diamonds appear colorless, while the rarest varieties have a hint of blue coloring.

༄10༄

Q What are some possible options for today's engagement ring?

A Probably the first consideration for a groom is whether to purchase a new engagement ring or present a family heirloom. The most traditional engagement ring is a diamond solitaire which can easily be paired with a variety of wedding bands. Some brides prefer to wear their engagement and wedding rings separately, or to just wear their engagement rings on special occasions.

∽11∾

*Q*Where should an engagement ring be purchased?

*A*Engagement rings can be found in jewelry stores and the fine jewelry department in some department stores.

∽12∾

*Q*What considerations should be made in choosing a jeweler?

*A*The bridal couple should visit several jewelers to compare selection of styles, workmanship, price points, and customer service. Check each jeweler's credentials and memberships in professional jewelry associations: this will be an indication of whether they are serious about their craft.

∽ 13 ∽

Q What is the benefit of a jeweler's membership in the American Gem Society?

A The American Gem Society, founded in 1931, is an organization maintaining high standards for its members, and sponsors ongoing educational programs to train retail sales associates.

∽ 14 ∽

Q What is a setting?

A The setting refers to the arrangement of stones within the metal frame of the ring. A good setting is like the right picture frame: it needs to show off what is inside and be able to fit in with its surroundings. It is, therefore, important to find the perfect setting that goes not only with the stone the couple choose, but also looks good on the bride's hand.

∽ 15 ∽

Q What are the most common jewelry metals for engagement settings?

A Engagement rings are popularly available set in gold and white gold. Silver is rarely used due to the fact that it tarnishes and therefore is not a good representation for a marriage. Platinum, a metal used for rings prior to World War I, is now popular again in the rings worn by almost one-third of today's engaged women.

Q What is the difference between 14 karat gold and 24 karat gold used in wedding jewelry?

A These numbers refer to the purity of the gold—24 karat is pure gold, while 14 karat is a blend with 14 parts gold and 10 parts of another metal.

∽17∽

Q How can gemstones be incorporated in an engagement ring?

A Some brides choose their birthstone or favorite gemstone in a setting enhanced with diamonds.

∽18∽

Q What is the significance of the garnet?

A Garnet, the birthstone of January, is regarded to symbolize eternal friendship. The garnet is a semi-transparent, dark red gemstone.

∽19∽

Q What is the significance of the amethyst?

A According to biblical folklore, this February birthstone is a symbol of faithfulness and sincerity. This gem is a clear purple or bluish violet quartz widely used in various types of jewelry.

Q What is the significance of the aquamarine?

A The March birthstone is a transparent blue, blue-green, or green gemstone. It is said to symbolize intelligence and courage.

~21~

Q What is the significance of diamonds?

A Diamonds, the birthstone of April, are believed to protect the wearer from evil spirits and represent innocence and matrimonial happiness. While most diamonds appear colorless, others offer a hint of color ranging from a soft blue to light yellow.

~22~

Q What is the significance of the emerald?

A The birthstone of May is a symbol of domestic harmony and success in love. This gem is a transparent green stone.

∞ 23 ∞

Q What is the significance of the pearl?

A The pearl is said to reflect health and longevity, and is the birthstone of June.

∞ 24 ∞

Q What is the significance of the ruby?

A The July birthstone, a red corundum, is the symbol of love and contentment. Legend suggests that a ruby engagement ring will darken in color if the course of true love is not running smoothly.

∞ 25 ∞

Q What is the significance of the sardonyx?

A Married happiness is expressed by the sardonyx, the birthstone of August. This gemstone is a white-and-brown variety of the onyx.

Q What is the significance of the sapphire?

A The sapphire is said to bring its wearer good health and good fortune. The birthstone for September represents truth and faithfulness. This gemstone is from the same family as the ruby, but is rich blue in color.

Q What is the significance of the opal?

A The October birthstone symbolizes hope. This gem is often marked with an iridescent mixture of colors against a soft, milky white ground or a vivid, fiery ground.

Q What is the significance of the topaz?

A Fidelity is expressed in the November birthstone, which is a yellow to yellow-brown transparent gemstone.

❧29❧

Q What is the significance of the turquoise?

A Turquoise, a blue, bluish-green, or green gem is the December birthstone. It is said to represent prosperity.

❧30❧

Q What criteria should a couple use in shopping for a diamond ring?

A The diamond industry has identified the four C's—color, clarity, cut, and carat weight—to assist consumers in making educated purchases.

❧31❧

Q What is color?

A The majority of diamonds do appear colorless, though there are many that contain a hint of color. The Gemological Institute of America has a letter grading system for classifying the color of diamonds, starting with D for the slightest blue tone and spanning the alphabet to Z for the yellow stones.

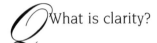

∞32∞

Q What is clarity?

A The clarity of a diamond refers to the number of internal flaws contained in the stone. Diamonds, the crystallized form of carbon, may contain some impurities that are often visible only by a jeweler's microscope. The fewer number of flaws increases the value of the stone.

∞33∞

Q What is cut?

A The cut of a diamond refers to the design of facets, including the round solitaire, marquise, oval, pear, and emerald. High-quality diamonds reflect more light and appear to have a greater sparkle.

34

Q What is a marquise cut?

A The marquise cut refers to a stone that is pointed at both ends.

35

Q What is the emerald cut?

A An emerald cut refers to a stone that is square or rectangular.

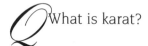

36

Q What is karat?

A The karat of a stone is a unit of weight for precious gems equal to 200 milligrams. There are 100 points to a karat.

37

Q What is the average size of a diamond engagement ring?

A The average size of an engagement ring today is about .75 karat.

38

Q Who pays for the groom's wedding band?

A It is usually the bride-to-be who purchases her fiancé's wedding band. The most popular groom's rings today are classic bands of gold or platinum.

39

Q How should couples determine how much to spend on a diamond ring?

A Financial experts recommend that couples spend not more than three weeks' salary, or roughly 6 percent of annual income. On the other hand, the jewelry experts recommend investing some two to three months income in the engagement ring.

Clearly, couples must set their own budget and not be overly influenced by industry advice. Couples with limited finances at the time of their engagement can certainly reset the stone or add extra stones at a later date.

40

Q What is the value of an outside appraisal?

A Before making the final purchase of an engagement ring, the groom should take the ring to an
independent appraiser for examination. The
appraiser will prepare a written document that
confirms the specific composition of both the
stone and the setting, including a detailed
description of the weight, color, and shape. The
appraisal essentially identifies the quality of the
ring, which should be compatible with the price
set by the jeweler. Any discrepancy in the
appraiser's examination of the stone and setting
should be resolved with the jeweler before the
sale is complete.

41

Q What customer service should a quality jeweler
provide after the purchase of an engagement ring?

A Most jewelers offer complimentary sizing, cleaning, and tightening of the stone for the first six
months or year of ownership.

☙42☙

Q Is extra insurance necessary to protect an engagement ring?

A For some couples, the wedding jewelry can be
covered on a basic homeowner's insurance policy,
but should be separately itemized listings. The
rings should be reappraised about every five years
and the insurance coverage adjusted to reflect the
current value.

Couples should consult with their insurance
agent to determine their needs—protection
against theft and/or loss, and coverage if the
whole ring is lost, not just the stone.

☙43☙

Q Once the bride and groom become engaged, how
should the engagement be announced?

A Both sets of parents should be the first to learn of
the upcoming marriage. Traditionally, the bride's
family hosts the first social gathering to share the
good news with family members and close
friends. If the groom's family resides in a distant
hometown, they may also host an engagement
party for the couple.

∞44∞

Q Is it necessary to have formal engagement announcements?

A After sharing the good news with the immediate family members and close friends, there will be other family members, friends, and colleagues who the couple will want to inform. A formal announcement is the most traditional vehicle for providing the information.

∞45∞

Q How should an engagement announcement be worded?

A

Mr. and Mrs. James Arthur Anderson
announce the engagement of their daughter
Caroline McLean

to

Mr. Charles Edward Hayworth
February the fourteenth
Nineteen hundred and ninety-eight

∽46∽

Q Are there any variations on the traditional engagement announcement?

A Although the complete date of the engagement is usually shown, some prefer to indicate just the month and year.

∽47∾

Q When should the official engagement announcement appear in the newspaper?

A Most newspapers prefer to announce engage-
ments between six months and one month before
the wedding day. The bride should contact the
newspaper(s) she wants the announcement in to
find their particular procedure and time.

∽48∾

Q What information should be publicized in the
newspaper engagement announcement?

A Most newspapers can provide the bride with a
standard form to complete with the following
information on both the bride and groom: first,
middle, and last names; names and hometowns
of parents; schools attended and degrees
received; current job title and employer; date and
location of wedding.

∽49∾

Q Should a couple expect to be billed for their
engagement announcement to appear in the
newspaper?

Although most newspapers historically printed engagement announcements as a courtesy to its readers, it is not unusual today for a nominal fee to be assessed for the publication.

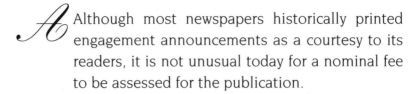

What is the usual guideline for the publication of an engagement photograph with the couple's formal engagement announcement?

Many newspapers will accept only professional photographs to publish with both engagement and wedding announcements. Some newspapers, however, are limited by space requirements to only accept one photo; couples will need to agree which announcement they prefer to accompany with a photo.

If the groom's parents reside some distance from the bride's parents, may they announce the couple's engagement in the groom's hometown newspaper?

The bride's parents should provide all the information necessary to announce the engagement in the groom's hometown. It is not traditional for the groom's parents to make the engagement announcement.

∞52∞

Q If the bride's parents are divorced, how should the engagement announcement be worded in the newspaper?

A Mr. James Arthur Anderson of Dallas, Texas, and Mrs. Laura Lee Anderson of Atlanta, Georgia, announce the engagement of their daughter Caroline McLean to Charles Edward Hayworth, the son of Mr. and Mrs. Mitchell Pines Hayworth of Kansas City, Missouri.

∞53∞

Q If the bride's parents are divorced, how should the formal engagement announcement be worded?

A

Mr. James Arthur Anderson
Mrs. Laura Lee Anderson
announce the engagement of their daughter
Caroline McLean

to

Charles Edward Hayworth
February the fourteenth
Nineteen hundred and ninety-eight

∞54∞

Q If the bride and groom are hosting their own wedding, how should the engagement announcement be worded in the newspaper?

A Caroline McLean Anderson, a graduate student at Boston University, is to be married to Charles Edward Hayworth, a doctoral candidate at Emory University in Atlanta, Georgia. Miss Anderson is the daughter of Mr. and Mrs. James Arthur Anderson of Dallas, Texas. Mr. Hayworth is the son of Mr. and Mrs. Mitchell Pines Hayworth of Kansas City, Missouri.

∞55∞

Q Are guests expected to bring gifts to an engagement party?

A Guests are never expected to bring gifts to an engagement party, but they often do.

∞56∞

Q Should the engaged couple open gifts given to them at their engagement party?

A Unless every guest attending the party brings a gift, the couple should open their gifts during a private moment.

◎57◎

Q Who offers the first toast to the engaged couple at their engagement party?

A The bride's father is the first to invite guests to raise their glass in honor of the bride- and groom-to-be.

◎58◎

Q How do the bride and groom respond to the bride's father's toast?

A As all the party guests drink their beverage, the bride and groom refrain from drinking. The groom-to-be then offers a toast to honor his fiancée and her family.

When the groom-to-be has concluded his short speech, other guests may propose toasts to the couple and their parents.

◎59◎

Q Who determines the guest list for the engagement party?

A The bride- and groom-to-be should be ready to provide names and addresses of their immediate family members and close friends for the hostess of the engagement party.

∽60∾

Q Is it customary for the bride-to-be to present her fiancé with an engagement gift?

A There is no requirement that the bride-to-be choose an engagement gift for her fiancé, although many engaged women give a personal, long-lasting present to their future husband. Popular gift choices include a watch engraved with the date or a special message, or a leather portfolio stamped with his initials.

∽61∾

Q What is the recommended length of a couple's engagement?

A Most couples plan a year-long engagement to make preparations for their wedding, although some of the most popular wedding specialists can be booked from 12 to 18 months in advance.

2

Beginning to Plan

∞62∞

Q At what point should the parents of the bride meet the parents of the groom?

A If both sets of parents have not had the chance to be introduced to each other just before the couple's announcement of their engagement, the bride- and groom-to-be should orchestrate such a meeting. Typically, the groom's family makes the initial gesture to become acquainted with the bride's family.

2

∞63∞

Q What is the first step that an engaged couple should undertake in planning their wedding?

A The couple should have a candid conversation between themselves about the type of wedding they both want and identify priorities for the entire wedding celebration. They should talk about dreams as well as realities and discuss their ideas with each set of parents.

∞64∞

Q How does an engaged couple determine the kind of wedding they want?

Family traditions and local customs along with the couple's personal style are the key factors that influence a couple's wedding planning.

It's a good idea to collect photographs and favorite ideas from the pages of **Elegant Bride**.

 65

Q What are the two primary styles of weddings?

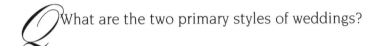 Most wedding celebrations are classified either as formal or informal.

66

Q What factors influence the formality of a wedding?

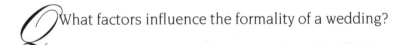 The degree of elegance of the ceremony and reception, along with the size of the wedding party and guest list are the most important elements. Once the degree of formality has been determined, the theme should be consistent throughout all facets of the wedding, including the invitations, attire, reception menu, decorations, etc.

∽67∾

Q How much time does it take to plan a wedding, and what makes the planning so complicated?

A The simplest wedding can no doubt be arranged with just a handful of telephone calls and meetings, while a more grand affair can take many months of planning. For most brides-to-be and their families, a wedding is the biggest and most important social occasion ever planned in a lifetime. It is a delicate blend of three special facets: a religious and/or legal ceremony, a wonderful party, and the formalized union of two families.

∽68∾

Q Is it acceptable for the bride to wear her engagement ring before the engagement is formally announced?

A The bride should enjoy wearing her engagement ring as soon as it is presented to her!

∽69∾

Q What factors should be taken into consideration when setting the wedding date?

A Many engaged couples like to schedule their wedding during their favorite season of the year, keeping in mind their work or school schedule, holidays, and the availability of their preferred sites for the ceremony and reception.

∞ 70 ∞

Q What superstition surrounds the selection of the wedding date?

A It was long thought that couples should marry on the waxing, not waning, moon to avoid bad luck.

∞ 71 ∞

Q What are the most popular months during which weddings take place today?

A May is the most popular month, followed closely by June, September, and October.

∞ 72 ∞

Q What day of the week is most popular for wedding celebrations?

A The most popular day for couples to marry is Saturday, followed by Sunday. In some of the larger metropolitan cities, a Thursday evening wedding is considered ultraformal.

∞73∞

Q When must a civil ceremony in a judge's chambers be scheduled?

A A civil ceremony performed by a judge in his chambers must take place on a weekday during regular office hours.

∞74∞

Q What factors influence the time of the wedding celebration?

A Traditionally, the timing of the marriage ceremony was influenced by religious restrictions. Couples of the Jewish religion traditionally marry after sundown on Saturday or on Sunday; they may not marry during the Sabbath between sundown on Friday and sundown on Saturday.

The most traditional Roman Catholic mass marriage ceremony is scheduled between eight in the morning and noon.

The officiant presiding over the marriage vows can provide expert advice regarding the selection of day and time.

∞75∞

Q What superstition surrounds the time of day that a couple marries?

A It was believed that the wedding ceremony should be held between the half hour and hour, when the rising hand of the clock was said to denote good fortune.

❧76❧

Q How does the time of day of the wedding celebration correlate with the formality of the occasion?

A A marriage ceremony scheduled at noon or after six o'clock in the evening is considered ultraformal. Morning and afternoon weddings are typically considered less formal.

❧77❧

Q What options can an engaged couple consider for the location of their marriage ceremony?

A A religious ceremony most often takes place in a house of worship, while religious and civil services can additionally be held in a hotel or public facility, a private home, or an outdoor location.

❧78❧

Q Is it necessary to invite wedding guests to both the marriage ceremony and the reception?

Traditionally, all guests are invited to the ceremony and the party that follows. However, it is not unusual for the exchange of vows to be witnessed just by the families and very close friends, with a larger guest list for the reception. Couples planning on a limited budget may opt to invite a large audience for the ceremony and host a modest reception at the same facility immediately following.

If the bride and groom opt for a destination wedding, is it acceptable for them to have a reception in their hometown after the honeymoon?

Many couples who return from a destination wedding are the guests of honor at a reception hosted by the bride's or groom's parents. Other couples may prefer to host an open house gathering in their new home for family members and close friends shortly after their return.

Is it appropriate for the bride and groom to don their wedding day apparel for the post-honeymoon reception?

A Yes, although the bride may opt to remove her veil for the party as well as bustle the train of her gown.

∽81∽

Q Is it possible for the family pet to have a role in the wedding?

A Even the most perfectly behaved pet may not be able to withstand the rigors of performing in the marriage ceremony, thus it's not a good idea for a pet to be assigned a meaningful role for the wedding.

A bride or groom who feels a special affinity for their pet should plan on having some pictures taken by the photographer at home with the pet before the festivities begin.

∽82∽

Q How can a couple avoid conflict related to any aspect of their wedding?

A The art of compromise becomes very critical to minimizing disagreements as the details of the wedding begin to come together. It is important to consider the needs and expectations of the bride and groom and their immediate families.

∞83∞

Q What are the most important steps to creating the wedding budget?

A The first step is to establish the immediate availability of funds to cover the expense of the wedding. Next, a couple should identify and prioritize all of the details they want for their wedding, and then begin to obtain price estimates.

∞84∞

Q What are the most common mistakes that couples make in creating their wedding budget?

A Since most couples have little or no experience in planning such a detailed event, it is not unusual for couples to underestimate the projected expenses for their wedding. And, once they are caught up in the excitement of the planning, it is not unusual for couples to bow to an appealing option that does not fit into their budget.

∞85∞

Q What are the sources of funds to help defray the cost of the wedding?

A Contributions to the wedding budget most often come from the parents of the bride, the bride-to-be, the groom-to-be, and the groom's parents. Sometimes grandparents or godparents will offer a donation to the budget.

Q How should a couple prioritize the details of their wedding celebration?

A The couple, along with each of their families, should create separate lists for the essential items, desirable details, and the extra finishing touches. Then the bride- and groom-to-be should look over these lists together and prioritize items in each list so that only the items they feel are most important are at the top of each list. Working from these lists, they can then obtain an estimate for each item and decide what they can and cannot afford.

∞87∞

Q What details are considered essential to the wedding budget?

A Essential elements of the wedding budget include the wedding day attire for the bride and groom, usage fees for the ceremony site, the cost of the wedding rings, plus the cost of the license, and the officiant's fee.

Q What details of the wedding budget are considered the desired elements?

A Other important facets of the wedding celebration include invitations, music for the ceremony and reception, flowers, photography, and videography.

Q What are the extra finishing touches that would enhance the wedding celebration?

A Special effects might include beauty pampering for the bride, a horse-drawn carriage or limousine to transport the newlyweds, calligraphy for the invitations, hospitality baskets for the out-of-town guests, and reception favors for all the guests.

∞ **90** ∞

Q What expenses does the bride's family typically assume for the wedding?

A The bride and her family traditionally cover the majority of the costs associated with the wedding, including her attire, usage fees for the ceremony site, the reception, invitations, flowers, music for the ceremony and reception, photography/video, gifts for the bridesmaids, a memorable gift for the groom, and his wedding ring.

∞91∞

Q Is the bride's family responsible for paying the lodging for out-of-town guests?

A Each out-of-town guest is responsible for his or her own transportation and accommodation expenses.

∞92∞

Q Does the groom's family pay for anything at the wedding? If so, what?

A According to tradition, the groom and his family pay for the bride's engagement ring and wedding ring, a wedding gift for the bride, gifts for the groomsmen, his wedding day attire, the rehearsal dinner, fees and travel expenses for the officiant, the marriage license, and the honeymoon. In some areas of the country, it is a popular custom for the groom to pay for the bride's bouquet and both mothers' flowers.

In light of the significant financial burden on the bride's family, a growing number of grooms' families are offering to help with the wedding expenses. Although it is acceptable for the groom's family to make a financial contribution, it is not expected that they do so.

⌒93⌒

Q What is the single most effective way to reduce the cost of the wedding?

A The sometimes difficult trimming of the guest list can help in reducing the cost and yet retain all of the details the couple deem important.

⌒94⌒

Q What is the financial responsibility of each of the bridesmaids and groomsmen?

A Each attendant must cover the cost of his or her wedding day attire plus travel and lodging expenses. Each member of the wedding party typically chooses a personal wedding gift for the bride and groom, although it is not unusual for the bridesmaids or the groomsmen to pool their resources and choose a larger, more expensive present.

Q Who is responsible for hosting a shower for the bride?

A It is considered in poor taste for the bride's imme-diate family to host her shower. The bridesmaids might together host a shower, as well as the aunts of the bride or friends of the mother of the bride.

More than "two" showers hosted for the bride is considered "too" many!

Q What techniques might the bride-to-be employ to keep organized with planning the wedding?

A Each bride-to-be must determine her own method for maintaining the many wedding details. Some brides choose to organize the details by computer, while others will create a notebook to hold notes and brochures.

∽97∾

Q What is the advantage of hiring a professional wedding coordinator?

A The services of a full-service wedding coordinator can range from working very closely with the bride in making each major decision to helping with just a few of the details. A professional wedding coordinator is an experienced party planner who can advise the bride on proper etiquette as well as the selection of wedding professionals.

∽98∾

Q What type of bride might most appreciate the benefits of working with a professional wedding coordinator?

A A wedding consultant is especially helpful to out-of-town brides and brides with extremely busy careers and lifestyles. For brides who want a unique wedding or brides with a specific budget, a professional party planner can secure the proper specialists to provide the desired services.

∽99∾

Q How should a professional wedding coordinator be compensated for her service?

A The professional coordinator may set an hourly fee for the time spent attending to details of the wedding or she may receive a percentage of the cost of the entire wedding.

∽100∽

Q What expectations should the bride have of her wedding consultant?

A A professional wedding consultant should give ample references from previous bridal parties and should be available to assist the bride with the last-minute details of the wedding as well as be on hand for the entire wedding ceremony and reception.

∽101∽

Q What gestures should the bride and groom express to demonstrate their appreciation to the professionals who assist with the wedding planning?

A Tokens of gratitude, including flowers, a framed picture of the newlyweds or the like, should be sent to any wedding professionals along with a heartfelt note of thanks.

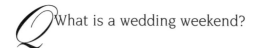

❧102❧

Q What is a wedding weekend?

A A recent trend that is growing quickly in popu-larity is the weekend wedding, including a series of parties along with the marriage ceremony and reception. With family members and friends traveling extensive distances to attend a wedding, a planned weekend allows a maximum amount of time for the bride and groom to visit with their guests.

❧103❧

Q What are some of the elements of a wedding weekend?

A There are no strict requirements for a weekend wedding except that all the participants enjoy each other's company. Many of the gatherings often center around mealtime entertainment and sporting activities as well as local sightseeing.

Among the possible parties are a barbecue or poolside party, a golf or tennis tournament, and a going-away brunch. Out-of-town guests may also be invited to the bridesmaids' luncheon, bachelor party, and rehearsal dinner.

∽104∾

Q Who hosts the weekend wedding functions?

A The bride's or groom's family may choose to host a special celebration in honor of the couple, or close family members or friends may offer to provide the hospitality.

∽105∾

Q How should the bride and groom plan their wedding weekend?

A As soon as the plans for an extended celebration begin to fall into place, the bride and groom should send a preliminary schedule of the festivities. Guests may need extra time to make their personal travel arrangements, so the notification should be a casual letter sent in advance of the wedding invitation.

∽106∾

Q If the bride's parents are hosting the wedding outside of their hometown, how can the bride help her family feel more like hosts and less like guests of the wedding?

Frequent communication to ask for advice and update parents on the plans will help them feel that they also have an active role in the wedding planning. The bride should send regular packages with information and photographs of the location or details so the parents can envision everything that will take place.

∞107∞

Q What are the legal requirements for marriage?

By law, all states require a marriage license and each state has its own regulations related to securing the license. The bridal couple should consult with the local marriage license bureau or county clerk's office in the county where the wedding will take place.

∞108∞

Q What questions are asked on the application for a marriage license?

The most common requirements are a certified proof of age and proof of citizenry. In addition, the bride and groom may need to submit a blood test and sustain a specified waiting period.

∞109∞

Q If a wedding is held in a foreign country, is it considered valid in the United States?

A In general, weddings held in foreign countries are recognized in the United States. The bridal couple should consult with the marriage license attorney in their hometown to determine the legal requirements.

∞110∞

Q How is the marriage license used in the wedding?

A Following the marriage ceremony, the honor attendants and the clergyperson will affix their signatures to the marriage license, which is later filed with the appropriate state or county agency.

3

The Bridal Party

∞111∞

Q What is the primary responsibility of each member of the wedding party?

A Although each member of the wedding party will have a different duty on the wedding day, the closest family members and friends should serve as a source of advice and support for the bride and groom.

∞112∞

3

Q What was the historic responsibility of the bridesmaids?

A The bridesmaids in ancient times were responsible for protecting the bride from evil spirits and serving as witnesses that she was not being married against her will.

∞113∞

Q What are the modern-day responsibilities of the bridesmaids?

A The bridesmaids are the sisters, cousins, and/or friends of the bride who take part in the wedding service and encourage the bride in the undertaking of marriage.

After the grandparents and the parents have been seated, and the groomsmen have taken their positions at the front of the church, the bridesmaids march in, one at a time, to join the men in the formation.

∞114∞

*Q*What are the financial obligations of the bridesmaids?

*A*The bridesmaids pay for their wedding day attire plus all of their clothes for the various prewedding parties. The maids will collectively entertain the bride with a luncheon or shower, and each bridesmaid will share in the cost. The bridesmaids are typically invited to all the prewedding parties and showers, where they must purchase a present for each occasion they attend as well as handle their own transportation and accommodations. Each bridesmaid will choose a wedding present for the newlyweds, or may join the other maids to pool their funds for a more significant gift.

∞115∞

*Q*What is the difference between a maid of honor and a matron of honor?

*A*The bride's honor attendant is distinguished by her own marital status: a maid of honor is an unmarried attendant and a matron of honor is a married attendant.

∽116∾

Q What are the responsibilities of the maid or matron of honor?

A The bride's honor attendant acts as her chief assistant by helping in any way that she is requested. She will likely accompany the bride to shop for the bridal fashions and will orchestrate the ordering and fitting of the maids' gowns. She will contribute to hosting a bridal shower.

On the wedding day, the bride's honor attendant helps the bride dress for the ceremony, carries the groom's wedding band, arranges the bride's train at the altar, and holds her flowers during the vows. She participates in the receiving line and sits next to the groom at the reception.

∽117∾

Q Is it acceptable for the bride to have two honor attendants?

A In cases where the bride has two sisters or two equally close friends, she may opt to have two honor attendants. These maids or matrons of honor share the traditional duties.

∞118∞

Q What was the historic responsibility of the best man?

A In olden days, abductors were known to skulk in the vicinity of a wedding, and harmful spirits were frequent, if uninvited, guests. It was the best man's responsibility to help shield the bride from abductors.

∞119∞

Q What are the modern-day responsibilities of the best man?

A In addition to offering his support to the groom, the best man assists the groom in selecting the formalwear for the men of the wedding party and organizes the ordering of each groomsman's attire. He helps the groom dress for the ceremony, carries the bride's wedding band, and offers the first toast at the reception. After the wedding, he collects all of the formalwear from the ushers for return to the rental shop and delivers the newly-weds' thank-you note and/or gift that expresses their warm appreciation to the bride's parents for hosting such a wonderful celebration.

∞120∞

Q Who may serve as the groom's best man?

A The groom's brother, cousin, or best friend are natural candidates for the role of best man. However, the trend of the groom's father taking this role is growing in popularity.

∞121∞

Q What are the responsibilities of the groomsmen?

A The groomsmen are the brothers, cousins, and friends of the groom who take part in the wedding and endorse the groom's choice of a life partner. They often lead the procession by walking to the front of the church just before the bridesmaids, and they usually escort the bridesmaids during the recessional.

∞122∞

Q What are the responsibilities of the ushers?

A The ushers are charged with welcoming the guests to the wedding and directing them to their seats in an orderly fashion. It is recommended that the groom plan on having one usher for every fifty guests.

In addition, the ushers distribute the wedding program, direct placement of the gifts, and sometimes escort the bridesmaids during the recessional and at the reception.

∞123∞

Q What are the financial obligations of the grooms-men and ushers?

A Each man is responsible for the rental fee of his wedding day formalwear. The groomsmen also attend all of the prewedding parties where they handle their own transportation and accommodations, plus select gifts for the events they attend. Each groomsman will choose a wedding gift for the bride and groom, or contribute to a large gift from all of the groomsmen.

∞124∞

Q Is it necessary to have an equal number of brides-maids and groomsmen?

A Although an equal number of male and female attendants assures the simplest configuration for the processional and recessional, it is not unusual to have extra groomsmen. The extra groomsmen may walk in single or double file as preferred by the bride.

∽125∽

Q When are young girls in the wedding party deemed junior bridesmaids?

A The young sister, cousin, or niece of the bride or groom becomes a junior bridesmaid if she is between nine and thirteen years of age. Typically, a junior bridesmaid will wear a dress similar to the bridesmaids.

∽126∽

Q What was the historic responsibility of the child attendants?

A The young girls and boys of ancient times sprinkled herbs and grains in the bride's path as a wish for her fertility.

∽127∽

Q What is the responsibility of the flower girl?

A The flower girl precedes the bride in the processional and scatters flower petals in her path. Or she may simply carry a small bouquet, basket, or wreath of flowers.

∞128∞

Q What is the responsibility of the ring bearer?

A The ring bearer is traditionally a young boy who either precedes or escorts the flower girl down the

aisle. He carries an embellished pillow to which the wedding rings are tied; typically, the rings attached to this pillow are symbolic and the honor attendants are charged with carrying the real rings.

∞129∞

Q What role does the father of the bride play?

A The father of the bride escorts his daughter to the front of the church and then "gives" her hand in marriage in the Christian service. In the Jewish tradition, both parents escort their son first and then their daughter to the rabbi.

∞130∞

Q Who may assume the responsibilities of the father of the bride?

A A bride may ask her brother, uncle, or close family friend to "give" her hand in marriage.

∞131∞

Q What role does the mother of the groom play?

A The mother of the groom is the first to be seated during the processional, after the grandparents. She additionally is the hostess of the rehearsal dinner party.

∽132∾

Q What role does the mother of the bride play?

A The mother of the bride is the last guest to be seated for the wedding, a few moments before the marriage ceremony begins, and is the official hostess of the wedding reception.

∽133∾

Q What role do the grandparents play?

A The grandparents of the bride and groom are very special guests of the wedding who often don new attire to the wedding party. The grandparents of the groom are seated before the grandparents of the bride. The bride and groom often include their grandparents when ordering corsages or nosegays and boutonnieres.

∽134∾

Q What role does the wedding director play?

A The wedding director is an unofficial member of the wedding party who makes sure that everyone is in his or her proper place throughout the wedding and reception. The wedding director is often honored with a corsage.

∞135∞

Q What considerations should the bride and groom make in choosing wedding gifts for their attendants?

A The tokens of gratitude given to the bridesmaids and groomsmen should be enduring treasures chosen with care. Some couples choose a gift that can be worn with the bridal attire on the wedding day.

The bride and groom should be sure to take enough time to prepare a personal, heartfelt note of appreciation to accompany the gift.

∞136∞

Q What are suggested gifts for the bride's wedding party?

A Pearl earrings, necklaces, or bracelets can complement almost any maid's attire. Other popular choices include gold jewelry, perfume holders, silk scarves, fine leather gloves, a crystal ring holder or paperweight, or an engraved sterling silver picture frame.

∽137∾

Q What are the suggested gifts for the groom's wedding party?

A Monogrammed cuff links make an ideal gift for the groomsmen. Engraved silver items are always a popular choice, including key chains, business card cases, or tankards. Elegant writing instruments are another favorite gift.

∞138∞

Q When should the attendants' gifts be presented?

A The rehearsal dinner is a perfect time for the bride and groom to turn the spotlight on their closest family members and friends in the wedding party. Other suitable occasions might be the bridesmaids' luncheon or the bachelor's party.

∞139∞

Q What was the traditional decorating of the newlyweds' getaway car by the wedding party?

A Tin cans tied to the back of a carriage were noisemakers to ward off evil spirits, and old shoes attached in a bundle represented the couple starting a new life together while leaving their old life behind.

∞140∞

Q What is the modern-day decoration of the newlyweds' getaway car by the wedding party?

A Although a few couples have trailing shoes and tin
cans attached to their cars, balloons and streamers are the most popular decoration.

4

Wedding Fashions

∞ 141 ∞

Q What characterizes a couture bridal gown?

A Couture, the French word for sewing, refers to bridal gowns constructed of exquisite fabrics, laces, and trims using the finest sewing techniques. These gowns often reflect the latest design trends in women's fashions.

∞ 142 ∞

Q What are the traditions behind the popular wedding rhyme "something old, something new, something borrowed, something blue, and a lucky sixpence in your shoe"?

4

A A bride often incorporates elements from this rhyme in her bridal attire: "Something old" is a symbol from the past, perhaps a family heirloom. These may include a treasured piece of jewelry, the family Bible, an embroidered handkerchief, or a bit of antique lace. "Something new" is a symbol of the future, and is most often chosen as the bridal gown. "Something borrowed" is often an accessory lent by a happily married woman, including jewelry, a veil, or a handkerchief. "Something blue" is inspired by the ancient Israelites to reflect love, fidelity, and purity, often visualized on the bridal garter. "A sixpence in your shoe" reflects the hope for good fortune and prosperity.

∞143∞

Q How soon should a bride begin shopping for her dream gown?

A Start the search as soon as the engagement is set, allowing at least four to six months for delivery and alterations of the gown and headpiece.

∞144∞

Q How does the bride determine what style of gown is best for her?

A The formality of the marriage ceremony that is being planned, along with the season and time of day of the scheduled festivities, determines the proper style of wedding gown.

∞145∞

Q How does a bride decide whether she should wear a white or ivory gown?

A Every bride should try on a range of gowns to decide the ideal shade that flatters her complexion and skin color. White can additionally refer to candlelight or winter white tones, and varies by choice of fabric.

∞146∞

Q What are the basic elements of a bridal gown?

A A bridal gown consists of an upper portion (bodice) and a lower portion (skirt) joined at the waistline. There are various styles of bodices that can be paired with numerous styles of skirts to form a unique bridal gown. Some bridal gowns have a train attached to the gown, varying in length.

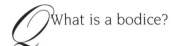

Q What is a bodice?

A The upper portion of a bridal gown, or bodice, which covers the torso and is made up of the neckline, shoulders, and sleeves.

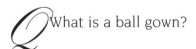

Q What are the most popular silhouettes of gowns for the bridal party?

A The most popular gown styles include the ball gown, Basque style, Empire gown, princess gown, sheath, A-line, and mermaid.

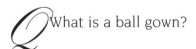

Q What is a ball gown?

A A ball gown features a fitted natural waist with a full skirt.

150

Q What is the Basque style?

A A Basque style has a tight-fitting bodice and dropped waist with V-front above a full skirt.

151

Q What is an Empire gown?

A The Empire gown features a cropped bodice and a high waist set just below the bustline.

∽152∾

Q What is a princess gown?

A A princess gown features vertical lines that flow from each shoulder to the hemline.

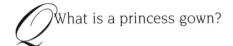

∽153∾

Q What is a sheath?

A The sheath is a body-hugging shape that follows a linear form without a waistline and with a straight skirt.

∽154∾

Q What is a mermaid?

A A mermaid is a variation of the sheath, distinguished by a trumpet skirt that extends below the knee.

∾155∾

Q What is an A-line?

A The A-line silhouette has a fitted bodice that steadily flares outward to the hemline.

∾156∾

Q What are the most popular hemlines of gowns for the bridal party?

The most popular hemlines include mini, street-length, midi, tea-length, ballerina, ballet-length, and floor-length.

 What is the mini-length and street-length?

The mini-length falls above the knee. Extremely short dresses are termed as micromini. A street-length dress falls around the knee, ranging from just above to just below the knee.

∞158∞

How do the midi and tea-length differ?

The midi-length dress falls above the midcalf, while a tea-length dress falls at the midcalf.

What is a handkerchief hemline?

A handkerchief hemline typically features a multitude of soft layers that fall in points at the tea-length, or midcalf, height.

∞160∞

Q What is the difference between the ballerina and ballet-length?

A The ballerina-length refers to a full skirt that ends just above the ankle. The ballet-length gown lightly brushes the ankles.

∞161∞

Q What is floor-length?

A A hem that falls just above the floor is termed floor-length.

∞162∞

Q What is a Watteau train?

A In contrast to the majority of trains that extend from the waistline, a Watteau falls from the shoulders.

∞163∞

Q What is a keyhole back?

A Some gowns feature a shaped cutout in the form
of a heart, teardrop, circle, or diamond that is
termed a keyhole.

❧164❧

Q What is a bateau neckline?

A A bateau neckline is a boat-shaped neckline that follows the collarbone.

❧165❧

Q What is a jewel neckline?

A A jewel neckline is a high, rounded neckline that circles the base of the neck.

❧166❧

Q What is a portrait neckline?

A A portrait neckline stands away from the body, usually framing the shoulders.

∞167∞

Q What is a sabrina neckline?

A A sabrina neckline is the same boatlike shape of the bateau, only placed closer to the base of the neck.

Q What is a scoop neckline?

A neckline shaped in a U is termed a scoop.

∞169∞

What is a strapless neckline?

 A strapless neckline is shaped to fall just above the bustline.

∞170∞

What is a sweetheart neckline?

 A sweetheart neckline is shaped in the form similar to the base of a heart.

∞171∞

What is a bishop sleeve?

A bishop sleeve is inspired from religious garb, with a flowing sleeve gathered in a wide cuff at the wrist.

Q What is a cap sleeve?

A A cap sleeve extends from the shoulder to subtly cover the top of the arm.

Q What is a gauntlet sleeve?

A A gauntlet sleeve is a full-length sleeve that extends over the wrist in a pointed V shape.

∽174∾

Q What is a leg-of-mutton sleeve?

A A leg-of-mutton sleeve has a large, fully rounded crown that tapers to a fitted wrist.

Q What is a petal sleeve?

A A petal sleeve is typically a short sleeve with layered panels.

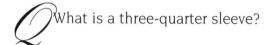

∞176∞

Q What is a three-quarter sleeve?

A A three-quarter sleeve falls just below the elbow.

∞177∞

Q What style of gown would enhance large hips or heavy legs?

A A gown with a full skirt minimizes heavy legs and hips; avoid straight styles and sheaths. A dramatic neckline helps to draw the eye upward and pull attention away from the hips, while an elongated waistline suggests extra height.

∞178∞

Q What style of gown would enhance a long, narrow body?

A A gown with a sleek bodice atop a full skirt with horizontal detail adds width; avoid high or dropped waists. The shoulder line becomes broadened with a gentle neckline or strapless gown, and a fitted waist creates feminine definition for a narrow form.

∽179∼

Q What style of gown would enhance broad shoulders or a large bustline?

A A gown with a simple, elegant bodice atop a skirt with special design interest helps to draw the eye downward; avoid narrow skirts and extremely high necklines. A modest neckline also reduces upper body width.

∽180∼

Q What are the different types of trains available on a wedding gown?

A A sweep-length is the shortest and lightly brushes the floor. The chapel-length extends about one and a half yards from the waist. For the most formal weddings, the cathedral-length train extends three yards from the waist.

∞181∞

Q What options are available to manage ease of movement with a train?

A Many trains are detachable and can be removed after the marriage ceremony for dancing at the reception. Many styles can be bustled, a gentle gathering of the train fabric that is fastened to the back of the waist.

∞182∞

Q What types of headpieces are available to accessorize a bridal gown?

A The most popular styles include stylish hats, romantic floral wreaths, and simple headbands. The most traditional headpiece includes a veil.

∞183∞

Q What are the different types of veils?

A Veils are typically classified by length, including elbow-length and fingertip-length. Many brides wearing gowns with trains choose a veil of the

same length, including chapel-length and cathedral-length. A pouf is constructed of gathered veiling attached to the back of the headpiece.

What is a blusher?

A blusher is a simple layer of veiling worn over the face before the ceremony and lifted back by the groom during the vows.

⌘185⌘

Q What factors should influence the choice of the headpiece?

A Considerations should include the style of wedding gown, the decorations on the gown, the shape of the bride's face, and her hairstyle.

Ideally, the neckline of the wedding gown should balance with the headpiece.

⌘186⌘

Q What is the importance of an underlining in the construction of a bridal gown?

A An underlining is affixed to the fashion fabric in order to add body and shape to a bride's or maid's gown. Many bridal gowns feature a colored underlining of pink, peach, or light blue that adds a hint of color to the garment.

⌘187⌘

Q What is boning and how is it used in bridal fashions?

A Boning is a construction technique intended to provide extra support, most often in a fitted bodice. A stiffening material—historically whale-bone, but currently plastic or metal—is inserted into narrow fabric channels and placed to create a smooth line throughout the torso.

∞188∞

Q What are the characteristics of satin fabric in bridal fashions?

A Satin can appear as a majestic fabric, used alone or in combination with other cloths, laces, and trims. Its pearl-like luster is achieved by its distinctive weaving of filling yarns carried on the surface of the fabric that provide a unique softness and sheen. Satin can be constructed of silk or synthetic fibers.

∞189∞

Q What is peau de soie?

A Peau de soie is a variation of silk satin characterized by a matte finish.

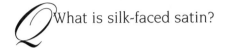

Q What is silk-faced satin?

A Silk-faced satin features silk fibers woven on the surface of a synthetic fiber base.

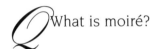

Q What is moiré?

A Moiré is a sturdy yet elegant fashion fabric characterized by a watermarked surface design. Although available in silk construction, it is most widely available in synthetic fibers. Moiré is the French word for watered.

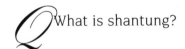

Q What is shantung?

A Shantung is one of the most widely used silk fabrics for bridal gowns, characterized by irregular slubbed filling yarns that contribute to a prominent horizontal dimension of the fabric.

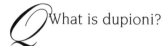

Q What is dupioni?

A Dupioni is a lighter variation of silk shantung, with threads of uneven size and weight spun together.

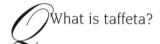

Q What is taffeta?

A Taffeta is a tightly woven, lightweight fabric which is known by its characteristic rustle and smooth, glossy texture.

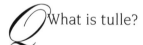

Q What is tulle?

A Tulle is a delicate fabric of fine netting, lightly layered to create veils and headpieces, or used in multiple layers to form full, ball gown skirts.

 196

Q What is velvet?

A Velvet is a soft fabric with a short pile, originally made of pure silk, but now more popularly available in a silk and rayon blend. The heavier weight of the fabric makes it most suitable for winter bridal and bridesmaids' gowns.

197

Q What is the most popular type of lace used in bridal fashion?

A Alençon lace is the most popular lace for wedding gowns, originating in northwestern France. The design typically features a floral motif outlined with a silken cord on a net background and is often re-embroidered to create a three-dimensional quality as well as embellished with pearls, beads, or sequins.

 198

Q What is Chantilly lace?

A Chantilly lace is similar to Alençon lace but without the cord outline. The construction is known for its subtle pattern and soft, delicate hand, and originates in northern France.

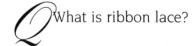

Q What is ribbon lace?

A Ribbon lace is created with the application of narrow ribbon to the lace motifs of either Alençon or Chantilly lace.

Q What is Guipure lace?

A One of the heaviest laces, Guipure lace is derived from silk-covered cords. It is often created as a series of intricate motifs that can be used whole as the fashion fabric or cut apart to form an edging detail or appliqué. The name dates back to the medieval French word "guiper" that refers to covering in silk.

Q What is Venice lace?

 Venice lace is a variation of Guipure lace that originated in northeast Italy.

∞202∞

Q What factors determine the price of a wedding gown?

A The cost of a gown is dictated by the amount and quality of fabric, the amount of beading or lace, and the necessary labor.

∞203∞

Q What is the standard payment procedure for bridal fashions?

A A bride should be prepared to place a 50 percent deposit on her gown at the time of her order.

∞204∞

Q How should a bride begin shopping for her wedding gown?

A After flipping through the pages of **Elegant Bride** to get some ideas, the bride should arrange appointments at several nearby salons. It will be helpful if the bride has a price range in mind before she begins shopping.

205

Q How close is the sizing of bridal gowns to the size ranges of other women's fashions?

A Since dress sizes vary slightly among the hundreds of bridal manufacturers, the bride-to-be should be most concerned with providing her exact measurements and trusting her bridal salon to order the appropriate size.

206

Q How much time should be allowed for delivery on a custom-ordered bridal gown?

A Delivery times do vary among manufacturers, and the bride should allow at least twelve weeks after placing her order and deposit. The bride should also allow time for local alterations with a goal of picking up her finished gown about two weeks before the wedding.

207

Q What is the standard practice regarding the cost of alterations?

A Although some salons offer custom fitting of the bridal gown as a complimentary service, the majority of salons do charge a fee ranging from $50 to $200 for alteration services. Extra charges could be added for storing and pressing the dress, as well as a fee for the protective garment bag.

☜208☞

Q What attire is appropriate for a semiformal wedding?

A A semiformal wedding usually calls for the bride to choose a floor-length gown with minimal decoration. A headpiece is optional. The groom and all of his groomsmen would each don a black tuxedo worn with a white pleated formal shirt, bow tie, vest, or cummerbund. The bridesmaids would choose floor-length or tea-length dresses accessorized with jewelry, hosiery, shoes, and optional gloves.

☜209☞

Q What attire is recommended for an informal daytime wedding?

A A street-length silk dress or dressy suit for the bride is a good choice for a less formal occasion. The groom may choose a dark business suit or a white dinner jacket with dress trousers for the summer or a tropical climate. The maids would choose simple, street-length dresses or suits similar to the bride's attire.

❧210❧

Q What fashion choices should be considered by an African-American bride for her wedding gown?

A The African-American bride may choose between wearing traditional African garments or may incorporate African motifs in contemporary styles. She may choose a classic wedding gown paired with an African-inspired headpiece or opt for a wrapped ensemble inspired by the traditional garb of the nation of her African heritage.

❧211❧

Q What fashion choices should be considered by an African-American groom for his wedding attire?

A The groom may choose between donning the traditional garb of the nation of his African heritage or he may incorporate the traditional kente or asooke fabrics in his wedding attire. Some formal-wear companies offer tuxedo jackets constructed of the traditionally patterned fabrics, or he may opt to wear a classic tuxedo accessorized with a tie, cummerbund, or scarf in the patterned fabric.

❧212❧

Q What is the appropriate attire for a second-time bride?

A Like all brides, the second-time bride should choose a dress that is correct for both the hour of the ceremony and the formality of the occasion. Trains and veils should be reserved for first-time brides, although she may wear a hat, bow, or flowers in her hair.

∞213∞

Q May a second-time bride wear white bridal finery?

A Old-fashioned wedding etiquette experts would agree that a bride who is remarrying should choose a gown in off-white or pastel-colored fabric. There is no rule that advises against wearing white, although many bridal fashion designers would urge the second-time bride to select ivory or a pale shade.

∞214∞

Q Who chooses the style of gowns worn by the bridesmaids?

A Traditionally, the bride selects the bridesmaids' attire. Many brides today will shop with their honor attendant and as many maids as possible to choose a gown that everyone appreciates.

❧215❧

Q If the bridesmaids live in several distant towns, where should their gowns be ordered?

A The bridesmaids' gowns are typically ordered at the same salon as the bride's gown. The salon can provide measurement cards for out-of-town attendants, order the appropriate size gown, and mail it to her in advance of the wedding.

❧216❧

Q What is the procedure for altering the bridesmaids' gowns?

A The bride should arrange a schedule for fitting the maids' gowns in plenty of time before the wedding to allow for alterations. Out-of-town maids will most likely secure a local seamstress to perform the task.

❧217❧

Q Who pays for the bridesmaids' gowns?

A Each maid is responsible for the cost of her gown and shoes.

218

Q Should the maids wear the same style of shoe?

A Although some brides attempt to save money by allowing each bridesmaid to select her own shoes, a more pleasing overall look will be achieved if each maid purchases the exact same shoe.

219

Q How should the bridesmaids' gowns be hemmed if the maids range in height?

A Dress hems measuring the same distance from the floor provide the most even and pleasing appearance. To achieve this, the tallest bridesmaid should have her dress hemmed and that same distance from the floor to the hem should be utilized by the entire wedding party.

220

Q Who chooses the attire for the flower girls?

A The bride typically chooses the dresses worn by the child attendants.

∞221∞

Q When should the children's outfits be purchased?

A Since young children are prone to unpredicted growth spurts, it may be wise to pick up their clothing about one month before the wedding.

222

Q Who pays for the outfits worn by the child attendants?

A The parents typically purchase the clothing their
child will wear in the wedding, although some
brides may choose to provide the attire as a gift.

223

Q What options are available for dressing the ring
bearer?

A While many brides opt to dress their ring bearer in
the same style formalwear as the men in the wedding party, a charming and perhaps more appropriate outfit is an Eton suit with short pants or
knickers. The choice of garment depends largely
upon the age of the ring bearer.

224

Q What should the mothers wear to a formal daytime wedding?

A Both mothers should wear tea-length or floor-
length dresses that complement each other in

style and color. The mothers' attire need not match the color scheme chosen by the bride for her maids, but should harmonize in shade and tone as well as degree of dressiness. The mothers may wear modest jewelry and gloves.

✇225✇

Q What should the mothers wear to a formal evening wedding?

A Both should wear floor-length or ankle-length ensembles. The gown styles and colors chosen by each of the mothers should blend with the formality of the bride's gown and the bridesmaids' attire. The mothers may select fancier accessories to accent their gowns, including elegant jewelry, handbags, gloves, shoes, and hosiery.

✇226✇

Q What should the mothers wear to a semiformal daytime wedding?

A Both should wear floor-length, tea-length, or street-length dress ensembles that are individually flattering and at the same time compatible with the dresses worn by the bridesmaids. The jewelry and fashion accessories selected to enhance their ensembles should be simple and understated.

◌∂227◌∂

Q What should the mothers wear to a semiformal evening wedding?

A Both should wear floor-length or ankle-length ensembles. The color, style, and dressiness of the mothers' gowns should coordinate with the attire worn by the bride and her maids.

∞228∞

Q What should the men of the wedding party wear?

A The degree of formality coupled with the time of day of the wedding festivities determines the appropriate attire for all the groomsmen.

∞229∞

Q Is it proper for the groom to wear a tailcoat while the groomsmen wear another style of jacket?

A All men of the wedding party wear identical formalwear. The groom can distinguish himself by a unique boutonniere.

∞230∞

Q What is appropriate men's attire for a formal daytime wedding?

A A formal daytime wedding requires that the gentlemen are dressed in classic cutaway coats with gray pinstripe trousers, gray vest, and ascot or four-in-hand tie. Optional accessories to complete the outfit include a top hat, spats, and matching gray gloves.

∽231∾

Q What is appropriate men's attire for a semiformal daytime wedding?

A A semiformal daytime wedding calls for a gray stroller with pinstripe trousers with four-in-hand tie. A stroller is similar in cut to a man's suit jacket with single-breasted front closure and squared hemline.

❦232❧

Q What is appropriate men's attire for a formal evening wedding?

A A formal evening wedding dictates black full dress coat with a white wing-collar shirt, white pique vest, and bow tie.

∞233∞

Q What is appropriate men's attire for a semiformal evening wedding?

A A classic tuxedo is the proper choice for a semi-formal evening wedding.

∞234∞

Q When is a white dinner jacket appropriate wedding attire?

A A white dinner jacket with formal trousers is suitable for nighttime celebrations in tropical climates.

∞235∞

Q Should the men of the wedding party buy or rent their attire?

A Although some men may own a tuxedo as part of their personal wardrobe, it will be unlikely that all of the groomsmen own the identical formalwear. A formalwear specialty store offers a wide selection of formalwear styles and can provide the customer service necessary to dress all the men in grand style.

236

Q How should the groom decide which formalwear he prefers?

A Once the type of appropriate formalwear is determined, the groom should try on several styles of jackets and trousers to decide what looks best. All coordinating accessories should also be rented from the same formalwear specialty store.

237

Q How does the groom arrange for formalwear rental for his out-of-town groomsmen?

A The formalwear specialist will provide measurement cards that can be mailed to out-of-town groomsmen. Each attendant should be professionally measured in his own hometown and return his sizes to the groom as quickly as possible.

238

Q When should the formalwear order be placed?

A The groom should allow at least three months before the wedding to ensure ample time for delivery and alterations.

239

Q What is the procedure for returning the rented formalwear?

A After the wedding festivities have ended, each groomsman will neatly assemble all the pieces of his attire and deliver it to the best man, who will return the outfits to the shop.

240

Q How can a groom personalize the wedding wardrobe of his groomsmen?

A The groom may opt to present a gift to each groomsmen of elegant cuff links and studs, a silk monogrammed handkerchief, or a pair of debonair suspenders.

241

Q What is the proper wedding attire for a groom serving in the military?

A A serviceman may choose to wear his dress uniform for the wedding.

∞242∞

Q If some, but not all, of the groomsmen are servicemen, what is proper dress for the gentlemen of the wedding party?

A The enlisted groomsmen would wear their dress uniforms and the other groomsmen would wear the traditional formalwear appropriate for the formality and time of the wedding celebration.

∞243∞

Q How should the grandfathers of the bride and groom dress for the wedding?

A Many bridal couples are inviting their grandfathers to don the same formalwear worn by the groomsmen and the fathers of the bride and groom.

∞244∞

Q Is it permissible for the groom to remove his jacket at the reception?

A Some grooms anticipate their need to feel comfortable at the reception and will have chosen patterned vests and ties for all the men of the wedding party.

ഛ245ഛ

Q How should the male guests dress for the wedding?

A Some couples invite male guests to dress in formalwear, although traditional etiquette recommends that all men wear formal attire to a wedding that commences at 6:00 P.M. or later.

ഛ246ഛ

Q What steps should be made for the preservation of the bride's gown?

A After changing into her going-away outfit, the bride should place her gown in a garment bag until she returns from the honeymoon and meets with her cleaner. The gown should be thoroughly inspected for stains.

ഛ247ഛ

Q What are the most common stains found on bridal gowns?

A Food and beverage top the list, followed by a soiled hemline, makeup and lipstick, and perspiration.

∞248∞

Q How should the bridal gown be packed after cleaning?

A The gown should be folded with sheets of acid-free tissue, and tissue should also be stuffed in the bodice to prevent permanent wrinkles and folds. The folded gown should be placed in an acid-free, lignin-free box designed for preservation.

∞249∞

Q Should the bride choose a preservation box with a mylar front that allows viewing of the gown in the box?

A Top gown preservation specialists advise against the use of a windowed box since it can contribute to yellowing of the exposed portion of the dress that is visible.

∞250∞

Q Where should a preserved gown be placed for storage?

A The best place to store a gown is in a cool, dry place such as underneath a bed, but not in an attic or basement where temperatures are too extreme. It is important that air is able to circulate around the box and provide a consistent, stable environment for the gown.

∞251∞

Q Once a gown is placed in a preservation box, can it be viewed without damage?

A The gown should be carefully taken out of the box every five to seven years and refolded to prevent permanent creases. White cotton gloves should be worn while handling the gown to protect the fabric from oily fingers or soil.

∞252∞

Q How can elements of an heirloom gown be incorporated into a wedding gown?

A An experienced seamstress can best assess the possible options of transferring either sections of the heirloom gown or simple pieces of lace to the new garment.

5

Wedding Jewelry / Accessories

∽253∾

Q What points should the bride consider when shopping for shoes for her wedding day?

A The material of the shoe should match the fabric of the bridal gown as closely as possible. The design of the shoe should complement the design of the gown, perhaps decorated with the same details as the dress.

Remember that a proper fit is critical to comfort.

∽254∾

Q Should the bride wear her bridal shoes before the wedding?

A The bride should break in her shoes during the week before the wedding, wearing them around the house on carpeted floors for a few hours each day.

∽255∾

Q How can a bride avoid tripping on slippery floors in her wedding shoes?

A In order to keep these shoes looking brand new, the bride can lightly apply fine sandpaper to abrade the smooth finish on the soles of the shoes.

∞256∞

Q How can a bride maximize the comfort of her wedding shoes?

A She should purchase a half-size larger shoe to wear on her wedding day and consider selecting a second style shoe that she can switch into during the reception celebration.

❧257❧

Q What factors should be considered when selecting bridal hosiery?

A The stockings should complement the style and fabric of the wedding gown, and vary according to sheerness, sheen, and pattern.

❧258❧

Q What types of designs are available in patterned hosiery?

A Patterned hosiery is available in allover designs as well as small, simple motifs positioned near the ankle.

❧259❧

Q What style of hosiery should be worn on the wedding day?

A The bride should choose patterned hose with plain, silk pumps and opt for simple hosiery to accent an embellished shoe.

∞260∞

Q What color of hosiery is appropriate for the wedding day?

A The bride should obtain a very sheer stocking that best matches the fabric of her wedding gown in white, ivory, or nude.

∞261∞

Q What types of headgear are available to the bride and her maids?

A In addition to the traditional veil, there are hats, headbands, floral wreaths, and combs.

∞262∞

Q What should the bride keep in mind while choosing her wedding day jewelry?

A The standard rule related to bridal jewelry recommends understated, simple, classic, and conservative themes. Most brides wear fewer, more formal pieces of high-quality wedding jewelry.

ꙮ263ꙮ

Q How should the bride's jewelry accent her wedding gown?

A The bride's jewelry, along with her other accessories, should reflect the formality of the wedding celebration. A small, informal wedding calls for simple jewelry, while a large, formal wedding calls for more elaborate jewelry.

ꙮ264ꙮ

Q What pieces of jewelry are considered most traditional?

A Diamond stud earrings suggest elegance, along with classic pearl necklaces and bracelets.

ꙮ265ꙮ

Q What jewelry is the most popular choice by brides?

A The symbol of purity and innocence, pearl jewelry is the most popular.

❧ 266 ❧

Q What are the different types of pearls used in wedding jewelry?

A The most prevalent types of pearls are cultured pearls, deep-sea pearls, and freshwater pearls.

❧ 267 ❧

Q What are cultured pearls?

A Cultured pearls are the most common variety of pearls, created by modern technology of inserting an irritant into the oyster to stimulate production.

❧ 268 ❧

Q What are deep-sea pearls?

A Deep-sea pearls are the naturally produced pearls.

Q What are freshwater pearls?

A Freshwater pearls are found in rivers and lakes, characterized by an irregular shape and color with intense luster.

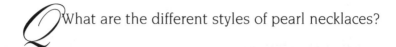

Q What are the different styles of pearl necklaces?

A The various lengths of pearl necklaces include the dog collar, choker, princess, mateneé, and opera.

∞271∞

Q What is a dog collar?

A A dog collar is made up of several strands of pearls stacked up on the neck.

∞272∞

Q What is a choker?

A A necklace that rests at the base of the throat is termed a choker.

Q What is a princess-length necklace?

A A princess-length necklace rests above the bust-line.

∞274∞

Q What is a matineé-length necklace?

A A matineé-length necklace rests below the bust-line.

∞275∞

Q What is an opera-length necklace?

A An opera-length necklace falls around the waist-line.

∞276∞

Q What is a lavaliere?

A pendant on a necklace is termed a lavaliere.

ᖇ277ᖉ

Q What types of gowns can be accessorized with a bracelet?

A Bracelets can be worn with sleeveless, short-sleeve, and three-quarter-sleeve gowns.

ᖇ278ᖉ

Q Is it possible to combine a bracelet with gloves?

A A bracelet can be a dramatic accessory worn over tight-fitted gloves.

ᖇ279ᖉ

Q Is it customary for the bride to wear a watch?

A Unless the watch is an unusual antique or family heirloom, most watches are not appropriate wedding jewelry for the bride or her maids.

∾280∾

Q What effect is achieved with a round, or button, earring?

A A button earring accentuates a round face.

∾281∾

Q What effect is achieved with a dangle earring?

A A dangle earring widens a narrow face.

∾282∾

Q What effect is achieved with a square- or emerald-shaped earring?

A A squared earring adds interest to a long face.

∾283∾

Q What kind of jewelry is appropriate for the bridesmaids?

A Most bridesmaid ensembles can be enhanced with earrings and perhaps a necklace or bracelet. All maids should wear the exact same jewelry.

Q How are gloves distinguished?

A Gloves are classified by length, measured by the number of inches, or buttons, the glove reaches above the thumb.

Q What are the various lengths of gloves?

A The most popular lengths of gloves include one-button, two-button, six-button, eight-button, and sixteen-button.

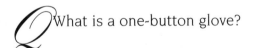

Q What is a one-button glove?

A A one-button glove stops just below the palm and is worn with long-sleeve gowns.

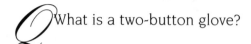

Q What is a two-button glove?

A A two-button glove ends at the wristbone and is also known as a wristlet or gauntlet.

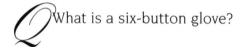

Q What is a six-button glove?

A A six-button glove falls below the elbow and is also known as a quarter-length glove. This style best accents a short-sleeve gown.

∞289∞

Q What is an eight-button glove?

A An eight-button glove reaches to the elbow and is worn with short-sleeve dresses.

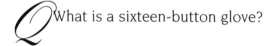

Q What is a sixteen-button glove?

A Also known as opera-length gloves, the sixteen-button glove reaches to the top of the arm. It is typically worn crushed, or gathered, and looks best with sleeveless or strapless wedding gowns.

∽291∾

Q What are the various types of gloves available to brides?

A Gloves can be made of kid leather, silk, matte cotton, crochet, and sheer.

∽292∾

Q How should a bride choose the color glove she wears with her wedding gown?

A White gowns dictate a white glove, while an ivory gown is paired with ivory gloves.

∽293∾

Q When should a bride wear gloves?

A The bride should wear her gloves for the processional and replace them following the marriage ceremony. She should wear them while greeting guests in the receiving line as well as dancing the special dances at the reception.

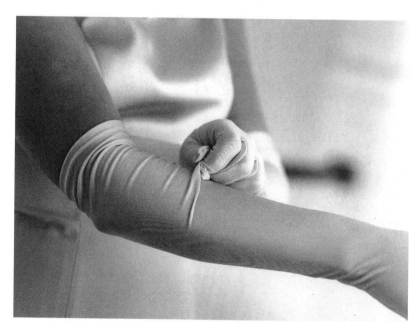

∽294∽

Q How does a bride handle the exchange of wedding rings if she is wearing gloves during the marriage ceremony?

A If she is wearing short gloves, she can simply remove her gloves and pass them to her honor attendant. Brides who opt for long, elbow-length gloves typically open the seams of the ring finger and tuck the fabric inside to expose the ring finger.

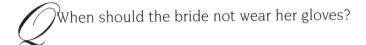

Q When should the bride not wear her gloves?

A The bride should remove her gloves while eating at the reception, to prevent possibility of any food stains on the gloves.

Q May a bride carry a handbag at her wedding?

A Most brides will use a handbag on their wedding day, but will never carry it down the aisle. The handbag is carried by the bride's mother or honor attendant.

❦297❦

Q What materials are most popular for the bridal handbag?

A Handbags are most often made of fabric or lace. Specialty bags may feature pearl and metallic trims. A bride wearing kid gloves may opt to carry on the look with a small leather handbag.

Q. May a bride carry a handkerchief?

A. Many brides receive a handkerchief as a bridal shower gift from an older female relative. The color should be white or ivory, and the bride's initials can be embroidered to personalize the practical accessory.

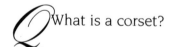

Q. What is the importance of wearing the proper undergarments with the bridal gown?

A. The proper undergarments will enhance the bride's figure and improve the fit of her gown.

300

Q. What is a corset?

A. A corset is a strapless bustier that fits to the waistline.

∞301∞

Q What is a merry widow?

A A merry widow is a corset with slightly longer length and garters to hold stockings.

∞302∞

Q Is it necessary for a bride to purchase a petticoat for her gown?

A Although some bridal gowns are constructed with the appropriate petticoat attached inside, many brides will want to purchase a petticoat to provide the desired fullness.

Brides interested in achieving a voluminous skirt may wear two petticoats.

6

Invitations /Stationery

∽303∽

Q What is the historical tradition of the wedding invitation?

A Centuries ago, the public announcing of banns by the church declared the intentions of those in a village who would soon marry. Today, the wedding invitation serves to spread the news with formality as well as the personal style of the engaged couple.

∽304∽

Q At what point in the wedding-planning process should the bride begin selecting the wedding invitations?

A Once the guest list has taken shape, the bride should schedule an appointment about four to six months before the wedding with a reputable stationer or obtain samples from the mail-order invitation specialists found in the pages of **Elegant Bride**.

6

∽305∽

Q In what cases is it proper to distribute handwritten wedding invitations?

A Invitations to a very small wedding may be handwritten personal notes written on plain stationery.

❦306❦

Q Is it possible to see a preview of the wedding invitation before the order is produced?

A Some, but not all, stationers do have the ability to provide a proof of the wedding invitation before it is printed for the bride to check for errors. The bride should ask about the availability of this service during her interview of the stationer.

❦307❦

Q When should the bride place the order for her wedding invitations?

A In order to leave enough time for engraving, proofreading, and addressing the invitations, a bride should try to place her order about four months before the wedding.

❦308❦

Q How much time should be allowed to prepare the invitations?

A A bride-to-be should allow at least ten weeks from the date the invitations are ordered until she puts them into the mail: the production of the invitation takes about six to eight weeks and the addressing of the invitations may take about two to four weeks.

309

Q Who pays for the wedding invitations?

A The bride's family traditionally bears the expense of all the wedding stationery, although the groom's family may wish to contribute if they will be extending more than half of the total number of invitations.

310

Q How soon before the wedding should the invitations be mailed?

A Standard wedding invitations are mailed about four weeks before the wedding. If the marriage has been scheduled during a holiday period, it is acceptable to mail the invitations about six weeks before the wedding.

311

Q When should invitations addressed to international locations be mailed?

A Couples should allow at least eight weeks for international mailings.

∞312∞

Q What is a save-the-date card?

A When a wedding is planned during a holiday or summer season, the couple may choose to send save-the-date cards in advance of the wedding invitations in order to facilitate the guests' ease of making travel arrangements.

∞313∞

Q What is the wording of a save-the-date card?

A Save-the-date cards are printed in a similar fashion as the wedding invitation:

Please save the date of
Saturday, the fourteenth of February
for the wedding of
Miss Caroline McLean Anderson
to
Mr. Charles Edward Hayworth

Mr. and Mrs. James Arthur Anderson

Invitation to follow

∽314∽

Q What factors contribute to the creation of the wedding invitation?

A The most important considerations will be the paper and the lettering or type style to be chosen.

∽315∽

Q With the virtually limitless array of wedding invitations available, how does a bride choose the best invitation?

A The invitation to a wedding should reflect the elegance and formality of the wedding celebration.

∞316∞

Q What factors contribute to the assembly of the guest list?

A The wedding budget coupled with the facilities for the marriage ceremony and reception will determine the number of guests to be invited.

∞317∞

Q What is the protocol for inviting colleagues from work to the wedding?

A It may be difficult to invite everyone from the office, and inviting just a few colleagues may result in bad feelings. If the entire group can't be invited to the wedding, the bride and groom should plan an open house or similar reception just for their professional associates to be held shortly after they return from the honeymoon.

∞318∞

Q How many wedding invitations should be ordered?

A In addition to the total number on the guest list, the bride-to-be should order extra keepsake invitations as well as a few for any last-minute guests. The guest list should include all members of the wedding party, the clergyperson and his or her spouse, and the fiancé(e) of any invited guest.

∞319∞

Q Once the total number of guests is established, how should the invitations be divided between the bride's and groom's family?

A The number of invitations are usually divided equally between the two families.

∞320∞

Q Is it necessary to invite the spouse of a relative or friend if they have never met the bride or groom?

A The invitations to married guests always include the spouse.

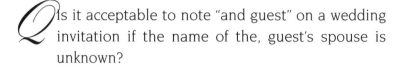

Q Is it acceptable to note "and guest" on a wedding invitation if the name of the, guest's spouse is unknown?

A The use of "and guest" should be avoided on all invitations. The bride-to-be or her mother should make the necessary inquiries to learn the proper names of the guests.

322

Q Is it necessary to invite guests to both the wedding and the reception?

A All guests who attend the marriage ceremony should be invited to the reception. If the ceremony site cannot accommodate the entire guest list, separate invitations to the reception should be addressed to other family members and friends.

323

Q What are the most popular styles of papers to choose for invitations?

A Traditional wedding invitations are made from either cotton or wood fibers. Those made from cotton are the most luxurious, with a rich, soft feel.

∞324∞

Q What are the most popular colors of papers to choose?

A White or ecru are the most appropriate colors for formal, traditional wedding invitations. Ecru, which is often also termed "buff" or "ivory," is the most popular choice of brides in the United States, while many European brides prefer white paper.

∞325∞

Q What is a "watermark"?

A If a paper held up to the light features a small, patterned design that is actually molded into the paper surface, that distinguishing symbol is known as a watermark. Watermarks date back to the eleventh century and were used to authenticate European church documents. In colonial times, Benjamin Franklin and George Washington used watermarks to personalize their own stationery. Today, a watermark is a symbol of high quality, and is not considered a blemish.

∞326∞

Q What is a "coat of arms"?

A Historically, a coat of arms was the regalia a knight wore into battle. The insignia has been translated into a small symbol unique to a family.

∞327∞

Q How is a coat of arms included on a wedding invitation?

A The insignia may be blind embossed at the top center of the wedding invitation. It is not proper to add color to the design.

The coat of arms can only be featured on wedding invitations sent by the families of the bride or groom; a bride and groom issuing their own invitation may not use a coat of arms.

∞328∞

Q What are the most popular sizes of wedding invitations?

A The most popular sizes range from 4 1/2" x 6 1/4" to the standard size of 5 5/8" x 7 1/2". Oversized invitations measure 6 3/8" to 8 7/8".

∽329∾

Q What is a letter sheet?

A Formal invitations that are folded on the left similar to a greeting card but without wording inside are known as a letter sheet.

∽330∾

Q What are the most popular styles of letter sheets?

A This type of wedding invitation can have a plain, smooth front or may feature an embossed single, double, or triple panel to frame the wording.

∽331∾

Q What is the difference between an engraved and a thermographed invitation?

A Engraving is the oldest and most refined printing method, where the text of the invitation is etched in reverse on a copper plate and then pressed with ink onto the paper. Thermography creates a similar look at a less expensive price by melting a powder over printed ink.

✎332✎

Q What is an easy way to determine if an invitation is engraved or thermographed?

A An engraved invitation will have a subtle indentation of each engraved line on the back of the paper.

✎333✎

Q Is there a proper color of ink used on wedding invitations?

A Traditional wedding invitations are always produced with black ink. The only exception is the use of dark gray ink, which can be substituted for some type styles that appear too heavy in black.

✎334✎

Q What elements make up the wording of a wedding invitation?

A The information on a wedding invitation includes the names of the hosts, the names of the bride and groom, plus the date, time, and location of the marriage ceremony.

∞335∞

Q What is the wording of a traditional wedding invitation?

A A traditional wedding invitation can be worded as follows:

Mr. and Mrs. James Arthur Anderson
request the honour of your presence
at the marriage of their daughter
Caroline McLean

to

Mr. Charles Edward Hayworth
on Saturday, the fourteenth of February
Nineteen hundred and ninety-eight
at seven o'clock in the evening
The First United Methodist Church
Dallas, Texas

∞336∞

Q Is it necessary to use the bride's or groom's complete name if they are not fond of their middle name?

A wedding invitation should not contain initials for middle names unless that initial is the full middle name.

∞337∞

Q Can nicknames by which the bride and groom are best known to family and friends be used?

A A formal wedding invitation requires the use of complete, formal names.

∞338∞

Q Can "junior" be abbreviated on a wedding invitation?

A The distinctive "junior" should be spelled out completely, preceded by a comma and with a lowercase "j."

∞339∞

Q What punctuation is allowed on a wedding invitation?

A The only use of punctuation is with the abbreviations "Mr. and Mrs." and when phrases requiring separation on the same line occur, as in the date of the wedding.

✆340✆

Q If the bride has a professional title, how should it be shown on her wedding invitation?

A Her full name is enhanced with the title of "Doctor" or "Judge" or the rank of her military status.

✆341✆

Q If the bride's father or the groom is a medical doctor, is it acceptable to use his title on the wedding invitation?

A Medical professionals may use the written "Doctor" with their names.

✆342✆

Q If the bride's mother is a medical doctor, is it acceptable to use her title on the wedding invitation?

A In the most traditional etiquette, the bride's mother would prefer to use her social title of

"Mrs." on her daughter's wedding invitation rather than her professional title. Today, however, some female doctors prefer to use their professional title, as follows:

Doctor Laura Lee Anderson

and Mr. James Arthur Anderson

request the honor of your presence

at the marriage of their daughter

Caroline McLean

etc.

∞343∞

Q If the bride, groom, or either of her parents has a Ph.D., how is it noted on the wedding invitation?

A Academic degrees are only used in academic settings and are not proper on wedding invitations.

∞344∞

Q If the bride's father is a minister, how should his name and title be noted on the wedding invitation?

A The top line of the wedding invitation should read, "The Reverend and Mrs. James Arthur

Anderson." If the bride's father is a minister who also holds a doctorate, the invitational line reads, "The Reverend Doctor James Arthur Anderson."

345

Q If the bride's father is a judge, how should his name and title be noted on the wedding invitation?

A The title "Judge" precedes his name.

346

Q What is the difference in the spellings of "honor" and "honour" and "favor" and "favour"?

A Honor" and "favor" are the American spellings for these words, while "honour" and "favour" are the English spellings. Virtually all brides prefer to add a touch of tradition to their wedding invitations with the English spelling of "honour" and "favour."

347

Q What circumstances determine whether the request line reads "requests the honour of your presence" or "requests the pleasure of your company"?

A The proper wording of a marriage ceremony held in a house of worship requires "requests the honour of your presence." Marriage ceremonies and receptions held in any location other than a house of worship requires "requests the pleasure of your company."

❧ 348 ❧

Q Is it necessary to include the year in the date of a wedding invitation?

A Since it should be obvious to the guests that a wedding is scheduled for the next month or so, it is not necessary to include the year. However, since the wedding invitation is a keepsake that may be saved as a special remembrance, it is acceptable to include the year with the date.

❧ 349 ❧

Q What are the proper ways to list the year on a wedding invitation?

A The year may be listed as "One thousand, nine hundred and ninety-eight" or "Nineteen hundred and ninety-eight."

∽350∾

Q How are half hours treated when listing the time on a wedding invitation?

A Half hours are written as "half after" the hour, never "half past" the hour.

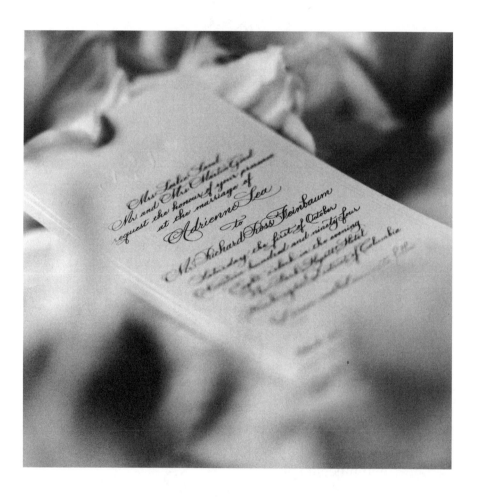

∞351∞

Q When must numbers be spelled out and when can the numeral be used?

A Numbers in a date are always spelled out. Long numbers associated with a street address may be written with numerals.

∞352∞

Q May the notation of "Black tie" be placed on the wedding invitation to suggest that male guests dress in formalwear?

A Since the time of day of the wedding and the location of the festivities determine the degree of formality of the guests' attire, it is not correct to add mention of "Black tie." It may, however, appear in the lower right corner of the reception card.

∞353∞

Q When is it appropriate to add the notation of "White tie" to a reception card?

A An ultraformal wedding celebration at which it is preferred that the gentlemen don tailcoats with wing-collar shirts and white tie may add the notation to the reception card.

༖354༗

Q If the bride and groom are paying for the majority of the wedding expense, should the invitation be extended in their name?

A The names of those inviting guests are placed on the top line of the wedding invitation, most often the parents of the bride. The invitation is not intended to report who is paying for the wedding.

༖355༗

Q If the parents of the groom make a sizable contribution to the expense of the wedding, is it proper for their name to be on the invitation?

A It is a modern-day trend for the groom's parents to be noted on a Christian wedding invitation, typically as appreciation for their assistance in staging the wedding. The groom's parents' names are always included on the invitation to a Jewish wedding.

༖356༗

Q What is the proper wording of an invitation to a Jewish wedding ceremony?

A The proper wording for a Jewish wedding invitation is:

Mr. and Mrs. Jacob Levy
Mr. and Mrs. Michael Adler
request the honour of your presence
at the marriage of their children
Amanda Beth Levy
and
Louis Scott Adler
Saturday, the fourteenth of February
at half after six o'clock
Washington Hebrew Congregation
Washington, District of Columbia

∞357∞

Q Is it necessary to use "at the marriage of their children" on an invitation to a Jewish wedding?

A Since there are some brides and grooms who feel that they are too old for this verbiage, it has become accepted to substitute "at the marriage of."

∽358∾

Q What is the proper wording of an invitation to a Nuptial Mass?

A A Nuptial Mass is a marriage ceremony that is performed as part of the Roman Catholic service, with special invitations:

Mr. and Mrs. Franklin Edward White

request the honour of your presence

at the Nuptial Mass at which their daughter

Sydney Alicia

and

Nicholas John Delano

will be united in the Sacrament of Holy Matrimony

on Saturday, the fourteenth of February

Nineteen hundred and ninety-eight

St. Patrick's Catholic Church

Hudson, Wisconsin

∽359∾

Q What is the proper wording of an invitation to a military wedding?

A An example for the wording to a military wedding is:

Mr. and Mrs. Frederick Giles Davis

request the honour of your presence

at the marriage of their daughter

Martha Jane

to

Captain Benjamin Ross Astor

United States Navy

etc.

∽360∽

Q What is the proper wording of an invitation to a double wedding?

A A double wedding may have an invitation worded something similar to this:

Dr. and Mrs. Kenneth Matthew Flynn

request the honor of your presence

at the marriage of their daughters

Laura Elizabeth

to

Ian Thomas Roth

and

Linda Ann

to

Phillip Scott Philcox

etc.

∽361∾

Q If the bride's parents are divorced, how are their names shown on the wedding invitation?

A The bride's parents' names are placed on two separate lines at the top of the invitation, with no conjunctive "and." In cases where the bride's parents are not friendly, the mother may issue invitations to the marriage ceremony and the father may issue invitations to the reception.

∽362∾

Q If the bride's parents are divorced, how is the bride's mother's name treated?

A If the bride's mother has not remarried, she uses her first, maiden, and married names. If she has remarried, she uses "Mrs." followed by her husband's full name.

∽363∾

Q If the bride's parents are divorced and her father has remarried, how is his new wife's name treated?

A Traditionally, the bride is given in marriage by her parents, pointing to the listing of only her mother and father. If the father of the bride is hosting the reception and sending separate invitations, his wife's name may be joined with his on the invitational line.

364

Q What is the wording of an invitation to the marriage ceremony issued by the bride's divorced mother who has not remarried?

A An invitation issued by the bride's divorced mother may be worded like this, leaving out the "Mrs." that denotes being married to the bride's father:

Laura Lee Anderson

requests the honour of your presence

at the marriage of her daughter

Caroline McLean

etc.

365

Q What is the wording of an invitation to the wedding reception issued by the bride's divorced father who has remarried?

A If the bride's father has remarried, the reception invitation may include his new wife by wording it as "Mr. and Mrs.":

Mr. and Mrs. James Arthur Anderson
request the pleasure of your company
at the wedding reception of his daughter
Caroline McLean

to

Mr. Charles Edward Hayworth
on Saturday, the fourteenth of February
Nineteen hundred and ninety-eight
The Mansion on Turtle Creek
Dallas, Texas

366

Q If the bride's father is deceased, how is his name treated on the wedding invitation?

A A deceased parent is never identified on the wedding invitation. He or she should be identified in the newspaper announcement of the engagement and the wedding as "the daughter of Mrs. James Arthur Anderson and the late Mr. Anderson."

367

Q What is the proper wording of a wedding invitation issued by the bride's widowed mother?

A An invitation for a bride's widowed mother is similar to one issued by a bride's divorced mother; however, the term "Mrs." is used in this instance:

Mrs. James Arthur Anderson
requests the honour of your presence
at the marriage of her daughter
Caroline McLean

etc.

∽368∾

Q How is the wording of the invitation issued by the bride's widowed mother adjusted when she is remarried?

A She uses "Mrs." followed by her current husband's name on the invitational line. Since her new surname is different than the bride's, the bride's surname is added on the fourth line of the invitation.

∽369∾

Q What is the proper wording of a wedding invitation to a ceremony held at the home of friends?

A When a wedding is being held at the home of friends, that information is added after the time of the wedding ceremony:

Mr. and Mrs. James Arthur Anderson
request the pleasure of your company
at the marriage of their daughter
Caroline McLean

to

Mr. Charles Edward Hayworth
on Saturday, the fourteenth of February
Nineteen hundred and ninety-eight
at seven o'clock in the evening
at the home of Mr. and Mrs. Richard Thacker
102 Decker Court
Dallas, Texas

∞370∞

Q Under what circumstances is it appropriate for the bride and groom to issue their own wedding invitations?

A If the bride's parents are deceased or if the bridal couple is more mature, they may issue their own invitations. This style is also prevalent when the bride's parents are estranged following their divorce or the ceremony is a second wedding for the bride. Depending upon the amount of detail of the celebration, the couple may choose between a more formal or less formal wording for their invitation.

∞371∞

Q What is the proper wording of a more formal wedding invitation issued by the bride and groom?

A A more formal invitation would include the line "The honour of your presence…" at the beginning:

The honour of your presence
is requested at the marriage of
Miss Caroline McLean Anderson

to

Mr. Charles Edward Hayworth

etc.

∞372∞

Q What is the proper wording of a less formal wedding invitation issued by the bride and groom?

A A less formal wedding invitation would begin with the bride's and groom's names:

Miss Caroline McLean Anderson

and

Mr. Charles Edward Hayworth

request the honour of your presence
at their marriage

etc.

❧ 373 ❧

Q What is the recommended style of invitations for a second wedding?

A Although invitations to second weddings have historically been less formal, there is no restriction on sending formal, engraved invitations to a second wedding that will be an elegant occasion.

❧ 374 ❧

Q How should a bride marrying for the second time list her name on the wedding invitation?

A Most second-time brides will use their first name followed by their maiden name as their middle name and their last name. Typically, neither the bride or groom use a title in front of their names.

❧ 375 ❧

Q May a mature bride use the title "Ms." on her wedding invitations?

A The title "Ms." should be reserved exclusively for business correspondence, and should never be used on a wedding invitation.

∞376∞

Q What other elements help to make up the wedding invitation?

A Other enclosures include a reception invitation, response card, pew card, "at home" card, and direction card.

∞377∞

Q What is the tradition behind using two envelopes with a wedding invitation?

A In ancient days when wedding invitations were delivered by hand, it was the custom to dispose of the outer, possibly soiled envelope in order to present a pristine invitation.

∞378∞

Q How is the outer envelope of a wedding invitation addressed?

A The outer envelope should contain the names of the invited guests and their address.

❦379❧

Q Is it proper to list a return address on the outside envelope?

A It's a very good idea to include a return address on the outside envelope in the event that the sender doesn't have the most recent address for a guest. The most traditional placement calls for the return address to be blind embossed on the back flap; the return address should not appear on the front of the invitation envelope.

❦380❧

Q How is the inner envelope of a wedding invitation addressed?

A Each guest's title and family name is noted on the inner envelope, along with the first names of the children invited to join in the festivities.

❦381❧

Q When is it proper to send an individual invitation to a child?

A Any guest over the age of eighteen should receive his or her own invitation, even if he or she is living at home with parents.

☜382☞

Q How is an invitation addressed to a couple when the wife has retained her married name?

A The husband's full name is followed on the same line by his wife's name: "Mr. Thomas Alan Finch and Ms. Diana Marie Kilburn."

☜383☞

Q How is an invitation addressed to an unmarried couple?

A The names of the two individuals are placed on separate lines, with the name that comes first alphabetically on the top line.

☜384☞

Q In what instances is it appropriate to include a separate reception card with the wedding invitation?

A When the marriage ceremony and the reception that follows take place in two different locations, a reception card with the time and place is engraved in the same style as the wedding invitations.

∽385∾

Q What is the proper wording of a reception card?

A The reception card features four lines, centered. The first line lists the occasion and is noted as a breakfast when scheduled before 1:00 P.M. and as a reception when scheduled after 1:00 P.M. The second line indicates the time and typically reads "immediately following the ceremony." The third line contains the name of the reception site, and the fourth line lists the address. The fourth line is omitted when the reception site is very well known, or when map cards are included with the wedding invitation.

∽386∾

Q Is it acceptable to send travel information along with the wedding invitations to out-of-town guests?

A Although it is considered proper to enclose an engraved accommodations card with the wedding invitation, most brides prefer to create a separate mailing in advance of sending the wedding invitation that contains suggested hotels, travel directions, and brochures with local points of interest.

∞387∞

Q What does RSVP stand for?

A "Répondez, s'il vous plait" is the traditional French verbiage to solicit a response to the invitation. "The favour of a reply is requested" is also correct.

∞388∞

Q Is it necessary to include response cards with the wedding invitation?

A Although the most traditional etiquette would prompt the wedding guest to send a handwritten note to the parents of the bride, today's busy lifestyle has given rise to engraved reply cards being included with the wedding invitation. The cards are engraved in the same style as the invitation and provide space for the names of the guests and their responses.

∞389∞

Q When a choice of entrées will be served at the reception, is it appropriate to list the choices on the response card for guests to indicate their preferences?

The response card should not be a menu card, and it is not considered proper to announce the meal choices. Most professional caterers should be able to project the amounts of food necessary to serve the guests.

 390

Q What date should be used on the response cards?

 Brides-to-be should list three weeks before the wedding in order to receive the response cards and tally the number of expected guests by two weeks before the wedding.

391

Q If the guests do not return the response cards in the requested time frame, is it acceptable for the bride or her mother to telephone the guests to learn if they plan to attend the wedding?

 Those guests who were not cooperative in returning their response cards promptly deserve any embarrassment in being called to obtain a response.

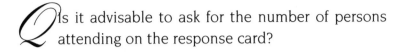

392

Q Is it advisable to ask for the number of persons attending on the response card?

A Since the hosts of the wedding have issued the invitation to a certain guest or family, they are fully aware of the number of guests attending. Such a notation might suggest to an unknowing guest that it is acceptable to bring additional guests, and thus it should be avoided.

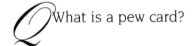

393

Q What is a pew card?

A Pew cards are sent with the invitations to guests who have been specifically assigned a pew at the church. The guest passes the pew card to the usher to be directed to the proper place for the marriage ceremony.

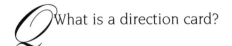

394

Q What is a direction card?

A A neatly drawn or printed local map that locates the sites of the ceremony and reception can be included with the invitation if many of the guests are from out of town or if the distance between the sites is considerable.

∞395∞

Q Is it acceptable to add a card noting the name of the store where the couple have placed their bridal gift registry with the wedding invitation?

A It is never considered in good taste to include with the invitation a card indicating where the couple are registered for gifts. Such a practice is acceptable only by the hostess of the bridal shower, who may include such a card for the convenience of the guests.

This information should be dispersed by word of mouth from the mothers of the bride and groom as well as the members of the wedding party.

∞396∞

Q Who should use the services of a calligrapher to address the various wedding stationery pieces?

A Busy brides-to-be who simply do not have time to address all the envelopes or who don't have attractive penmanship should enlist the services of a professional calligrapher. Also, calligraphy denotes a feeling of sophistication for formal wedding celebrations.

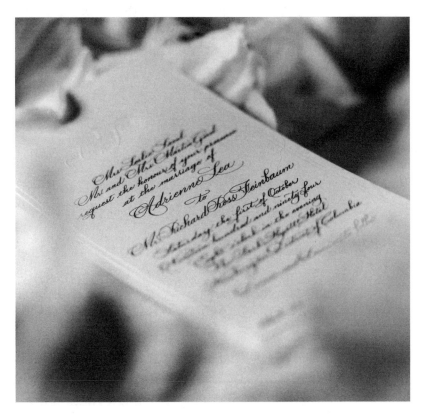

☙397❧

Q Is it necessary to include the tissue with the wedding invitation?

A Placing a small, white tissue over the wedding invitation dates back to the colonial era when slow-drying inks had a tendency to smudge on a newly printed paper. While some brides enjoy the

historical tradition and include the protective tissues over the invitation and each enclosure, it is
not necessary.

Brides who choose not to include the protective tissues should consider requesting that the
post office hand-cancel their invitations to reduce
the chance of smudging.

Q How are the various elements of the wedding invitation arranged in the inner envelope?

A Each supplemental piece should be stacked on
top of the wedding invitation by size with the
smallest piece on top. A typical arrangement
might be: the wedding invitation, the reception
invitation, the response card set beneath the flap
of its envelope, the map card, and the pew card. If
arranged correctly, the recipient should be able to
remove the entire contents of the invitation from
the inner envelope with the right hand and read
them without turning the cards around or over.

◌◌399◌◌

Q How is the inner envelope inserted into the outer
envelope?

A The front of the inner envelope should face the back of the outside envelope.

∽400∾

Q What kind of postage stamps should be used on the wedding invitations?

A The post office offers a selection of novelty stamps that are appropriate for the reply envelopes and the wedding invitations, including self-adhesive stamps that help to make the assembly process easier. The entire sealed invitation should be weighed to determine the correct amount of postage.

∽401∾

Q What is a wedding program?

A A growing number of brides-to-be are designing wedding programs to be distributed to guests upon their arrival at the marriage ceremony. The multipage program contains the order of service and identifies all the members of the wedding party. It is fashioned in the same style as the wedding invitations, and may feature the couple's monogram or a liturgical symbol on the cover.

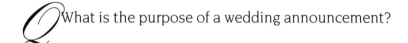

402

Q What is the purpose of a wedding announcement?

A Wedding announcements are traditionally sent to family members and friends not invited to the wedding, but with whom the bridal couple want to share news that the wedding has taken place.

403

Q How is a wedding announcement prepared?

A It is printed in a similar fashion to the wedding invitation, and is mailed on the day of or the day after the marriage. Like a wedding invitation, it is placed within two envelopes.

404

Q Who issues the wedding announcements?

A At a traditional wedding, it is customary for the parents of the bride to issue the wedding announcements. It is also acceptable for the bride and groom to issue their own announcements.

∽405∾

Q What is the proper wording of a wedding announcement issued by the parents of the bride?

A When the bride's parents are issuing the wedding announcement, their names are placed on the first line:

Mr. and Mrs. James Anderson

have the honour of announcing

the marriage of their daughter

Caroline McLean

to

Mr. Charles Edward Hayworth

Saturday, the fourteenth of February

Nineteen hundred and ninety-eight

The First United Methodist Church

Dallas, Texas

∽406∾

Q What is the proper wording of a wedding announcement issued by the bride and groom?

A When the bride and groom issue their own wedding announcement, the bride's and then the groom's names are at the beginning of the announcement:

Miss Caroline McLean Anderson

and

Mr. Charles Edward Hayworth

announce their marriage

Saturday, the fourteenth of February

Nineteen hundred and ninety-eight

The First United Methodist Church

Dallas, Texas

∽407∽

Q What are "at home" cards?

A An engraved card with the newlyweds' new address and the date they will be settled helps to make it easier for family members and friends to stay in touch after the wedding.

∽408∽

Q When should "at home" cards be mailed?

A They are small enclosure cards that are designed in the same style as the wedding invitation, and may be included with the invitation or with the announcement.

⤖409⤖

Q What is the proper wording for an "at home" card sent with the wedding invitation?

A The wording for an "at home" card can be simply done with just the date the bride and groom will be in their new residence and the address:

At home

after the first of March

200 Beech Lane

Fairfax, Virginia 22033

⤖410⤖

Q What is the proper wording for an "at home" card sent with the wedding announcement?

A An "at home" card sent with the wedding announcement is more formally done by beginning with the newlyweds' married names on the first line:

Mr. and Mrs. Charles Edward Hayworth

200 Beech Lane

Fairfax, Virginia 22033

after the first of March

∞411∞

Q How much time can a bride take to write thank-you notes?

A Many brides mistakenly assume that they have a year to acknowledge gifts. In truth, gifts received before the wedding should receive acknowledgment within two weeks, while gifts received after the wedding should be recognized within three months.

∞412∞

Q When should the bride order stationery for her thank-you notes?

A While the ceremony and reception sites are still being confirmed, a bride-to-be can select personal stationery for thank-you notes six or more months before the wedding.

∞413∞

Q What is the most popular style of stationery for thank-you notes written before the wedding?

A The most popular stationery for engaged women to write thank-you notes for bridal shower presents and early wedding gifts is the traditional, fold-over note engraved with her maiden name.

414

Q If the bride chooses to use single-initial notes for thank-you notes written before the wedding, which of her names should the initial represent?

A The majority of brides-to-be choose single-initial notes representing their maiden name.

415

Q What is the most popular style of stationery for thank-you notes written after the wedding?

A After the wedding, brides should use stationery engraved or embossed with her new monogram, or engraved with her new name. Since she will use this notepaper for much of her correspondence in years to come, she should take advantage of the savings offered by placing a large order.

416

Q If the bride plans to hyphenate her maiden and married name, how is her new monogram designed?

A A new monogram with four initials features the two initials of her maiden and married last name in the center with a hyphen, flanked on the left by the initial of her first name and on the right by the initial of her middle name.

∽417∽

Q Is it proper to have informal notes engraved with the couple's name, i.e., "Mr. and Mrs. Charles Edward Hayworth"?

A Traditional etiquette recommends that since the informals will be used primarily by the bride for her thank-you notes, that the notation read "Mrs. Charles Edward Hayworth." Stationery with the name of the married couple should be reserved for informal invitations issued by the couple.

∽418∽

Q What kind of stationery should be used if the groom will share in the task of writing thank-you notes?

A Since men do not write on fold-over notes, the groom should order a set of correspondence cards engraved with his own name.

∽419∽

Q When is it appropriate to send gift acknowledgment cards?

A If the newlyweds will be taking an extended honeymoon or if the bride will find it difficult to promptly write her thank-you notes, it is advisable to alert guests of the receipt of their gift with an acknowledgment card.

∞420∞

Q How is a gift acknowledgment card worded?

A A gift acknowledgment card simply states the bride's name and the receipt of the gift with an intention of writing:

Mrs. Charles Edward Hayworth

has received your very kind gift

and will write you later of her appreciation

∞421∞

Q If an emergency causes the wedding to be postponed after the invitations have been mailed, what should be done to notify guests?

A If there is enough time to have a document printed and mailed, the bride's parents would order postponement announcements in the same typeface as the wedding invitations:

Mr. and Mrs. James Arthur Anderson
announce that the marriage of their daughter
Caroline McLean

to

Mr. Charles Edward Hayworth
has been postponed from
Saturday, the fourteenth of February

until

Saturday, the sixth of June
at seven o'clock in the evening
The First United Methodist Church
Dallas, Texas

If there is not enough time to have these cards printed and mailed, the same message should be wired to out-of-town guests immediately and telephoned to local guests.

∽422∽

Q How is the cancellation of a wedding handled?

A If time allows to print and mail a formal announcement, it is worded:

Mr. and Mrs. James Arthur Anderson
announce the marriage of their daughter
Caroline McLean

to

Mr. Charles Edward Hayworth
by mutual agreement
will not take place

7

Flowers

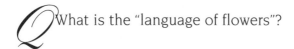

∞423∞

Q What is the "language of flowers"?

A The hidden meaning of flowers offers a special dimension to the wedding decorations. As an example, for a tribute to absent friends, the bride might choose a nosegay of zinnias for the church or reception.

∞424∞

Q Is it advisable for a friend or relative to create the floral decorations for the wedding?

A Unless the friend or relative is in the profession, it is generally advisable to leave the floral designing to professionals.

∞425∞

Q How much time before the wedding should a bride-to-be select the florist?

A Brides-to-be should begin interviewing potential florists as soon as the date of the wedding and the locations of the ceremony and reception are set.

Some florists only take one wedding booking per day, so it's a good idea to confirm as early as possible.

⤢426⤣

Q What traits should a bride-to-be look for in choosing the florist?

A She should pick a florist who is experienced, creative, and flexible enough to create the special touches she envisions for her wedding. Recommendations from friends, relatives, business co-workers, or acquaintances who are familiar with a florist's work are very helpful. The bride should request a list of references of recently married brides who can attest to the florist's talents.

⤢427⤣

Q Where can a bride-to-be find ideas for her wedding flowers?

A The pages of **Elegant Bride** are a perfect source of ideas about wedding flowers, with stories and photographs of a wide variety of floral details.

Attendance at a bridal fair will usually provide an opportunity to view the work of several local florists and the bride can arrange a follow-up appointment with the preferred floral professionals.

∽428∾

Q What are some of the historical traditions of wedding flowers?

A Roman brides wore fragrant wreaths of lemon verbena which they picked themselves on their wedding day, and in ancient Greece the wedding day was a flower-filled occasion for which the entire wedding party was crowned with blossoms.

∽429∾

Q What are some of the historical symbols of wedding flowers?

Pimpernel in a bouquet signals a change of life, while carnations speak of a woman's love. White daisies, white violets, and white lilacs radiate innocence. Forget-me-nots are the sign of true love, and ivy represents friendship, fidelity, and matrimony.

☙430❧

Q What is the significance of the orange blossom?

A The orange blossom has the unusual ability to produce fruit as well as bear flowers simultaneously, which was taken as a symbol for the fusion of beauty, personality, and fertility.

☙431❧

Q What is the general rule of thumb regarding all wedding flowers?

A The bride and her florist should work to coordinate all of the floral accents. All of the flowers should complement the season, the wedding gown, the ceremony, and reception site, as well as the personal style of the couple.

໑ 432 ໐

Q How can ribbon enhance the wedding flowers?

A A new dimension to an all-white bouquet can be achieved with the addition of a colored or textured ribbon. A unique effect can also be obtained with the use of hand-painted or antique ribbon.

໑ 433 ໐

Q What factors influence the type of bouquet carried by the bride?

A The bridal bouquet should complement the bride's wedding day attire. The style of the gown, coupled with the formality of the wedding, are the primary considerations in choosing the style, shape, and color of the bride's bouquet.

໑ 434 ໐

Q What is the practice of passing flowers to both mothers at the marriage ceremony?

A Many brides are asking their florists to arrange two loose flowers in her bouquet for the purpose of passing a flower to each mother. On her way up the aisle the bride offers one to her mother, and on her way back as a new bride she gives one to her new mother-in-law. This custom is a tender tribute to the two women who will play a very important role in her married life: the bride's mother who raised her and assisted with the wedding planning, as well as the groom's mother, who raised him and now welcomes her into his family.

☙435☙

*Q*How should the bride carry her bouquet?

The bride should act like her bouquet is a very weighty object so that her arms are extended, down in front of her.

∞436∞

Q Does the bride actually toss her wedding day bouquet at the end of the reception?

A More and more brides are choosing to preserve their wedding bouquets and are asking their florist to create a separate nosegay to toss to the single women friends at the conclusion of the reception.

∞437∞

Q What factors affect the type of flowers carried by the bridesmaids?

A When the bridesmaids are dressed in festive printed gowns, the best choice of flowers is a monochromatic bouquet colored in undertones of the fabric. Solid-color ensembles allow the bride's choice of a single floral tone or a combination of her favorite shades.

❧438❧

Q What information should the bride-to-be bring to her meeting with the florist?

A Once the selection of the florist is made and plans for the wedding are being discussed, the bride-to-be should carry swatches of fabric from her gown and the bridesmaids' dresses as well as pictures of bouquets and floral touches she admires. Specific details about the setting of the ceremony and reception will assist the florist in making recommendations about decorations.

❧439❧

Q How might a wedding scheduled on Valentine's Day or Mother's Day affect the bride?

A These holidays are particularly active for florists, and the competition for and the price of flowers is higher. In addition, a busy florist will have even less time and energy to devote to personally overseeing all the flowers for the wedding.

∽440∾

Q What factors affect the price of flowers at the wedding?

A Most flowers are available throughout the year from various flower-growing regions around the world. If a bride-to-be chooses flowers that are not easily available from local markets, the florist may be required to secure a more distant source, adding expense in the shipping of the blooms.

∽441∾

Q What factors influence the choice of flowers for the marriage ceremony?

A The ceremony site may be governed by certain restrictions regarding the use of flowers and decorations, as well as the times available for the installation of the decorations. The bride-to-be should check with the wedding coordinator at the church or synagogue for instructions.

∽442∾

Q What is the primary rule related to choosing flowers for the ceremony?

A Keeping in tune with the time of the ceremony and the respective formality, the flowers placed in a church or synagogue should enhance the beauty of the interior design and architectural details, while not overpowering the purpose of the occasion.

∽443∾

Q How should the ceremony flowers be chosen with respect to the bride's personal sense of style?

A While flowers provide such natural beauty, the floral decor at the wedding site must reflect the bride's good taste. Simplicity is always a symbol of beauty and elegance.

∽444∾

Q What considerations should be made regarding the altar decorations?

A The flowers for the altar should be chosen with respect of any objects that are a permanent part of the altar. In addition, the bride-to-be and her florist should gauge the amount of room available for the wedding party at the front of the sanctuary before filling the area with flowers.

⧼445⧽

Q What style of floral design is the most acceptable in a house of worship?

A Symmetrical balance is the most popular standard for arranging flowers in a church or synagogue.

⧼446⧽

Q What factors affect the style of floral decor in a house of worship?

A Since guests will be viewing the decorations from some distance, the arrangements should be chosen with appreciation for the proper size, density, and design. When planning more than one color or variety of flower in an arrangement, the stems should be chosen so they blend into each other.

⧼447⧽

Q What are some suggested color schemes for ceremony flowers?

A A predominantly white theme for the ceremony flowers lends attention to the beauty of the wedding party. Simple color harmony of a few shades of wedding flowers is typically more attractive than multiple tones.

∽448∽

Q What parts of the church or synagogue might be enhanced with flowers?

A Many brides-to-be opt for several formal floral arrangements on the altar plus floral touches for the front, kneeling bench, window sills, and pillars. The ends of the pews can be decorated with floral sprays or simple bows. In addition, the front door of the house of worship and the steps can be dressed with flowers or greenery and ribbon as well as the foyer.

∽449∽

Q How might the pews be decorated?

A The aisle may be dressed with flowers on every row or on alternate rows. The bride may chose to mark just the rows reserved for the immediate family.

∽450∾

Q What types of containers should be used to hold the flowers in a house of worship?

A Some churches and synagogues own floral holders like altar vases, standing baskets, or candelabrum that are for the use of the florist. The wedding director can advise on the availability and previous use of such containers.

∽451∾

Q Is it possible to use the same flowers for the ceremony and the reception?

A Although it can be done, most brides prefer to order separate arrangements for the church or synagogue and reception site. Otherwise, the guests may be greeted with undecorated tables at the reception while they wait for the florist to transport the flowers from the ceremony.

∽452∾

Q What factors influence the choice of flowers at the reception?

A The number of tables necessary to seat guests along with the layout will determine the number and style of centerpieces required. A knowledgeable florist will design arrangements that will not impede the beauty of the setting or the guests' ability to converse.

Additional floral accents can be designed for the place card table and cake table, plus chosen to enhance special architectural features of the setting. The entrance and foyer of the site may be decorated with flowers, as well as the powder rooms.

∽453∾

Q How should the bride-to-be enlist the creativity of her florist in designing the reception flowers?

A The bride-to-be and the florist should study the chosen reception site together and discuss the planned elements of the celebration. She should consider the colors that will be emphasized at the marriage ceremony, the type of food service, and the schedule of events in order to determine the most creative floral accents.

The florist should consider the most abundant flowers available for the season as well as which blooms would be hardy to last throughout the party.

∽454∾

Q What element of the reception decor might be the first display seen by the guests?

A The guest registry table is typically placed near the entrance to the reception and beautifully enhanced with the placement of a tasteful floral arrangement beside the guest book.

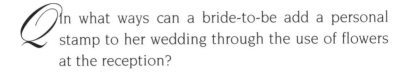

455

Q In what ways can a bride-to-be add a personal stamp to her wedding through the use of flowers at the reception?

A By adding an array of floral touches made up of her favorite blooms throughout the reception site, the bride will project her personal style as well as the formality of the celebration.

In addition to decorating the reception room, she may also add a welcoming touch with accents of flowers in the foyer and in the powder rooms. Some brides additionally choose to present each female guest with the gift of a small nosegay or single stem of flowers.

456

Q What is the symbolism of a flower circlet?

A Flower circlets carried by hand or floral crowns worn on the head represent the unbroken circle of the rings exchanged in the marriage service and symbolize eternal love and friendship. Flower circlets are particularly appealing for flower girls, who become adoringly accessorized with the addition of a floral crown to their wedding finery and who find carrying a floral hoop easier than a tiny nosegay.

☙457☙

Q What is a pomander?

A A pomander is a sphere of flowers carried by a ribbon handle, often a popular alternative for the flower girls.

☙458☙

Q What alternatives do the mothers have to wearing a corsage?

A Many mothers have long opted to attach flowers to their handbag, although today's mothers are carrying single roses tied with ribbon, miniature bouquets, or a small cluster of flowers tucked into a "tussie mussie," the Victorian-inspired, silver flower holder.

☙459☙

Q In what ways can flowers enhance the food service at the reception?

A With the intent of making the food look as wonderful as it tastes, the florist should join forces with the caterer. Together, the two might adorn trays of hors d'oeuvres with greenery or edible flowers. Buffet tables can be graced with fashionable topiaries or oversized arrangements placed in stately urns.

❧460❧

Q What is the rule of thumb regarding the design of centerpieces for the dining tables?

A The centerpieces should be either low or above eye level so that no one's view is cluttered and conversation is not impeded.

❧461❧

Q What role does the scent of the flowers play at the reception?

A Since the bride is interested in presenting a fragrant, floral display, she should take care not to be overpowered by any one particular flower.

❧462❧

Q Who is responsible for providing the flowers for the wedding cake, the cake baker or the florist?

A The bride-to-be should ask her florist to provide the cake accents for the cake baker after the three have agreed on the style of the cake and its decorations.

∝463∝

Q How should the cake table be decorated?

A Floral garlands or fresh greenery are a dainty accent for the cake table.

∝464∝

Q What is a boutonniere?

A A French term for "buttonhole," the boutonniere is the groom's floral accent on the lapel of his jacket.

∝465∝

Q What is the historical tradition of the boutonniere?

A The grooms of ancient Rome crowned themselves with wreaths of greenery on their wedding day. Later, the boutonniere evolved as a small, fragrant nosegay attached to the groom's wedding clothes before he took his place for the marriage ceremony.

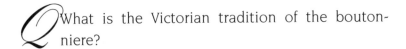

466

Q What is the Victorian tradition of the boutonniere?

A In the Victorian era, a groom wore a boutonniere
that was a single bloom from the bride's bouquet
as a symbol of her true love.

467

Q What is the Edwardian influence of a boutonniere?

A A simple gardenia pushed through the buttonhole reflects the charming elegance of the
Edwardian era.

468

Q What are the most popular choices of flowers for
boutonnieres?

A A single rosebud or carnation makes a traditional
statement, as does three perfect stephanotis
flowers. A sprig of white lilac is charming, simple,
and sweet.

∞469∞

Q What are some other elegant flower choices for the boutonniere?

A The groom might consider a spray of freesia against a dark green leaf or a pretty peach rose with aromatic eucalyptus leaves.

∞470∞

Q What is a typical springtime boutonniere?

A A single bridal white rose surrounded by cascading bells of lily-of-the-valley can be inspired by the bride's bouquet.

∞471∞

Q What is a typical summertime boutonniere?

A Colorful grape hyacinths, white daisies, or a single, vibrant gerbera daisy reflects the warm-weather months.

∞472∞

Q What style boutonniere is best at a December holiday wedding?

A The groom's wearing of a sprig of mistletoe gives him the perfect excuse to kiss the bride all day long.

∞473∞

Q Who traditionally wears a boutonniere?

A All of the men in the wedding party don a boutonniere, including the groom, his best man, the groomsmen, ushers, ring bearers, fathers, and grandfathers.

Traditionally, the groom is distinguished by a boutonniere that is slightly different and larger than the other gentlemen's boutonnieres.

∞474∞

Q When is it appropriate to distribute honorary boutonnieres?

A Brothers of the bride or groom who are not in the wedding party may wear a boutonniere to show their relationship and importance to the bride and groom.

❦475❦

Q What are other ideas for floral accents?

A Just about any object related to the wedding can be decorated with flowers, including the limousine or carriage that carries the newlyweds from the church or synagogue to the reception site.

❦476❦

Q What are some ideas for floral guest favors?

A Some brides opt to present each female guest with a flower. A small vase with a tiny nosegay or just a single flower can be set at each place setting at the reception. A sachet of fragrant potpourri can be distributed to all the women at the wedding.

❦477❦

Q What are some floral alternatives to the tossing of confetti?

A Some brides prefer to be showered by fresh rose petals or by potpourri.

∽478∾

Q What are some options for preserving the bride's bouquet?

A After treating the flowers in the bouquet, some florists rearrange the blooms in their original form to be placed in a glass box or on the shelf of a curio. Some brides prefer to have flowers from their bouquet accent a framed original of their wedding invitation.

479

Q How would the flower alstroemeria be used?

A This inexpensive striped variety of the lily family is available year-round as a wonderful filler flower for bouquets and arrangements. It is available in ten colors, ranging in yellow, peach, red, purple, pink, and lavender tones, and is well suited in both casual and high-style designs.

480

Q Where would the flower anemone be used in a wedding ceremony or reception?

A This spring bulb can be included in floral arrangements or used alone as a centerpiece. It's available in deep blue, red, pink, and white gossamer petals surrounding a dark center.

481

Q Can the aster be used in the bridal bouquet?

A This colorful, yet inexpensive, summer flower works well in bouquets as well as arrangements, and is available in deep or light purple, lavender, shocking pink, or white.

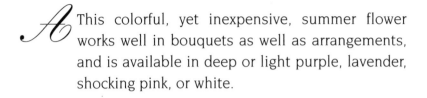

∽482∾

Q How can the azalea be used in floral decorations at a wedding?

A While the azalea is not suited to bouquets, it is a fine choice for a potted centerpiece or tucking branches into an arrangement. Azaleas are available in light and dark pink plus white.

∽483∾

Q Is the flower calla from the lily family?

A This springtime flower is often called a calla lily, and while it really is not a lily it does share many of its qualities. It is a traditional, long-lasting, elegant flower that truly makes a high-style statement. It can be found in white, yellow, rust, purple, and pink. The calla creates a dramatic image when featured alone in a bouquet or set in a simple vase, and is stunning arranged in clusters.

❧484❧

Q When are camellias available, and can they be used in a bouquet?

A These three-inch pink or white flowers can be wired in a bouquet or added to an arrangement. The simple, smooth blossoms and the fluffy double variety are seasonably available, primarily during the spring months.

❧485❧

Q How can carnations be used in the wedding ceremony?

A Perhaps one of the most popular and most versatile flowers, carnations are available in a full range of color and can be used in virtually any wedding flower design. They are long-lasting, fragrant, and inexpensive.

❧486❧

Q How do florists use chrysanthemums?

A This flower can be used as a filler in a tiny variety, as a dramatic statement in standard size, or the fine-petaled spider mum. They are long-lasting, inexpensive, and available year-round in a wide range of color.

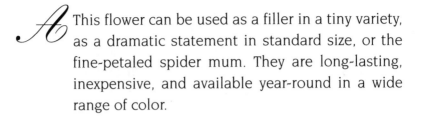

⌀487⌀

Q Are daffodils suitable wedding flowers?

A This sunny yellow spring bulb flower can be cut for bouquets or arrangements of planted bulbs for a centerpiece. It is an inexpensive flower during its own springtime season, and expensive when imported from Holland during other times of the year.

⌀488⌀

Q What is the significance of the daisy?

A The daisy is a symbol for innocence and hope. It is a natural-looking choice in bouquets and arrangements. Some brides request a traditional daisy chain, a garland of long-stemmed daisies tied together in a rope, for the bridesmaids or flower girl to carry.

✂489✂

Q During what season is the delphinium available for use in a wedding?

A This traditional wedding flower is available in spring and summer in shades of light or deep blue, white, and hybrid varieties of purple.

✂490✂

Q Can the freesia be used as a main flower?

A Freesia is a delicate, fragrant flower grown in ten colors that is often used as a filler in bouquets and arrangements added to other larger flowers. Single, separated blooms can be used in boutonnieres.

✂491✂

Q What is the significance of the gardenia?

A The gardenia is a pure white, highly fragrant flower that is the symbol of purity. It can be expensive, as it is sold per bloom. The gardenia was an extremely popular wedding flower of the 1950s that is enjoying a resurgence today.

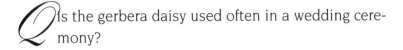

492

Q Is the gerbera daisy used often in a wedding ceremony?

A A wide range of color and availability year-round has increased the popularity of the gerbera daisy in both traditional and high-styled designs. It can be found in pink, deep rose, white, peach, red, purple, or yellow.

493

Q How would a florist use ginger in a wedding ceremony or reception?

A This exotic, tropical blossom is suited to altar decorations and banquet buffet table designs. It has a fiery red, burgundy, red, or pink bloom at the end of a slender green stem that is also found in a hanging variety.

494

Q What is the favorite use of the gladiolus in wedding flowers?

A This inexpensive flower is available year-round and dramatic in large floral sprays, or as individually plucked blooms for corsages and boutonnieres. It can be found in a full spectrum of color ranging from white to shades of red, pink, amber, yellow, and orange.

༄495༄

Q What is the significance of Hyacinthus?

A In Greek mythology, Hyacinthus was a young man loved by all who was tragically and accidentally killed by Apollo, a Greek god. He was memorialized by having the hyacinth flower grow in the area where he died.

Wonderfully fragrant in soft hues of creamy white, pink, light and deep blue to deep purple, this springtime bulb flower can be used whole in a garden setting arrangement for the altar or reception, or cut into individual flowers for a bouquet.

༄496༄

Q Can the iris be used in wedding floral arrangements?

A A predominantly springtime bulb flower, the iris is relatively inexpensive and available year-round. The orchid-like bloom makes a dramatic statement when used alone or in a small cluster, and makes a stunning touch to basket bouquets, hand clutches, and table designs. Known for its rich blue color, the iris is also available in purple, white, and yellow.

⌒497⌒

Q What is the significance of the lily?

A Depicted in Renaissance paintings as the symbol of purity, the lily can be found in a full range of color throughout the year, including pink, white, yellow, gold, and bronze. The blooms are long-lasting, dramatic, fragrant, and elegant.

⌒498⌒

Q Is the lily of the valley too delicate for wedding flowers?

A These tiny, pure white, bell-shaped blooms are both exquisite and expensive. They are often added to bouquets for a romantic elegance, or used in hair adornments and boutonnieres.

∞499∞

Q When would the flower lisianthus be used in a wedding ceremony or at the reception?

A Known as "Texas belles," these white, purple, or pink flowers offer an elegant, yet casual look to spring and summer bouquets and arrangements. A bouquet holder with water is necessary for a hand-held bouquet of these soft-petaled, half-dollar sized blooms, which look a bit like morning glories.

∞500∞

Q What is the best use of magnolia at a wedding?

A A traditional flower predominant in the South during the months of April through June, these large, fragrant blooms are most suitable for altar or reception arrangements.

∞501∞

Q Besides in a bouquet, how could an orchid be used in a wedding?

The first choice for a floral accent on a Bible, the orchid is a classic wedding flower that is also a favorite for a bridal bouquet, corsage, or boutonniere. Available throughout the year, the most popular varieties are the Cymbidium and the Dendrobium.

∞502∞

Could the pansy ever be used in the wedding flowers?

These brightly colored, summertime flowers are best presented in pretty pots at a reception. They are small and short-lived, but dramatic in "fresh from the garden" displays.

∞503∞

During what season could the peony be used?

These large, delicate flowers signal the beginning of summer in May or June. They are available in white as well as shades of pink or fuschia surrounding a dark center, and suggest a casual tone in arrangements.

⌒504⌒

Q What is the significance of the pineapple?

A The symbol of warm hospitality, flowering pineapples can be included in the reception decorations in centerpiece arrangements or in decorative accents around the room.

⌒505⌒

Q How can Queen Anne's lace be used in a wedding arrangement?

A This lacy, delicate flower adds a romantic flair to bouquets and arrangements. It is available in spring and summer to add texture and romance to wedding arrangements.

⌒506⌒

Q What is the significance of the rose?

A One of the nation's favorite flowers and a symbol of true love, the rose has been developed in a complete rainbow of colors available year-round. They may be used in a variety of stages, from formal, tightly budded blooms to large, casual blossoms that are similarly devoted to offering an air of casualness. Roses evoke an element of romance at a wedding, either as the feature flower or in combination with others.

Q What colors does statice come in?

A This tiny, inexpensive flower can be found in white, yellow, light blue, lavender, and deep purple.

508

Q Where can stephanotis be used?

A An extremely popular wedding flower, this fragrant, pure white bloom is versatile for any purpose in the wedding decorations. The five-petaled, trumpet flower is somewhat expensive, but an elegant detail in bridal bouquets, corsages, boutonnieres, and arrangements.

509

Q How does a florist use stock?

A This inexpensive, sturdy flower is used as filler and comes in about ten colors year-round.

510

Q Would the sunflower ever be used in a wedding?

A This summertime bloom is similar to a daisy, but with rich golden-yellow petals around a brown center. It is best suited to altar and reception

arrangements, and has enjoyed increased popularity in recent years.

∞511∞

Q How would a florist use the tulip?

A These delicate flowers have been developed in a
complete range of colors and add a dainty touch
to either a bouquet or table centerpieces. Their
hollow stems require the use of a bouquet holder
to provide water, which can be artfully concealed
under wrapped satin ribbon.

∞512∞

Q In which season can the zinnia be used in a wedding?

A A popular flower in the summertime, the zinnia
offers vivid color in bouquets and arrangements.
This inexpensive filler flower adds warmth to floral designs, available in white, yellow, red, orange,
and various shades of pink.

8

Music

❧513❧

Q Why is it important to choose the musical selections for the marriage ceremony with great care?

A The music of the wedding sets a memorable tone for the wedding party as well as the guests, serving to heighten the emotions of the occasion, and helping to create a permanent remembrance of the celebration.

❧514❧

Q What is the first step a bride-to-be should take related to choosing music to accompany the marriage ceremony?

A During one of their meetings with the clergyperson who will marry them, the engaged couple should inquire if the church or temple has a list of restrictions on music. Some houses of worship may prohibit the playing of certain tunes or may limit the use of instruments.

❧515❧

Q Who is the first person to consult with regarding the music for the ceremony?

The head organist of the church or temple will prove to be an invaluable source for the ceremony music-planning process. He or she will be able to relate the successes and failures of previous brides, as well as take the time to familiarize the couple with the most popular tunes.

8

∽516∾

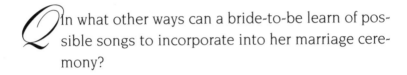 In what other ways can a bride-to-be learn of possible songs to incorporate into her marriage ceremony?

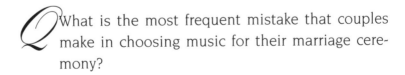 Local music stores and religious bookstores often carry tapes and CDs of popular wedding music. Most public libraries also have a selection of tapes for loan.

In addition, the bride should consult recently married family members and friends to learn of their musical selections.

∽517∾

What is the most frequent mistake that couples make in choosing music for their marriage ceremony?

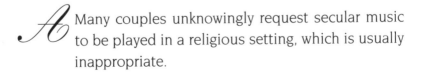 Many couples unknowingly request secular music to be played in a religious setting, which is usually inappropriate.

∞518∞

Q What are the most common ways to enhance the marriage ceremony with music?

A Most brides will choose a musical program that includes a prelude, processional music, service music, and recessional music.

∞519∞

Q What is a prelude?

A The prelude is the music that is played or sung before the wedding begins. Many brides design a program of songs that begin about thirty minutes before the ceremony as guests are being seated.

∞520∞

Q What is processional music?

A Processional music is the music played as the wedding party enters the sanctuary.

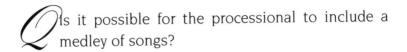

Q Is it possible for the processional to include a medley of songs?

A The bride-to-be may opt to distinguish the various members of the wedding party, with separate tunes for the seating of the grandparents and mothers, the entrance of the bridesmaids and groomsmen, and the entrance of the bride.

Q What is service music?

A Music used during the actual marriage ceremony is termed service music. These selections should be limited to just a few special tunes. Most popular after the vows are "Ave Maria" or "The Wedding Song." Some brides prefer a musical rendition of "The Lord's Prayer."

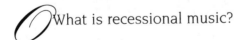

Q What is recessional music?

A Recessional music is the music played as the wedding party leaves the sanctuary, and continues as the guests depart. These selections should provide a lively, triumphant spirit.

∞524∞

Q Is it necessary to have the ceremony musicians participate in the wedding rehearsal?

A It's a good idea to conduct the complete wedding program, including all the music, during the rehearsal.

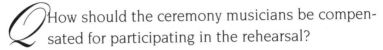

525

Q How should the ceremony musicians be compensated for participating in the rehearsal?

A The bride-to-be should be certain that the musicians' time to play at the rehearsal is included in the agreed fee.

526

Q What various musical elements add distinction to the wedding service?

A A trumpeter adds flair to the processional, while a harp, flute, violin, or guitar sets a romantic tone for the prelude. A string ensemble or children's choir lends a special touch to the ceremony.

527

Q What unique musical flavor should be considered in planning a holiday wedding?

A Appropriate seasonal selections are a natural choice for a holiday wedding.

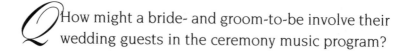

528

Q How might a bride- and groom-to-be involve their wedding guests in the ceremony music program?

A Many couples choose to include the singing of congregational hymns in the wedding service as a means of drawing their guests into the ceremony.

529

Q How can a bride-to-be find additional musicians and vocalists to accompany the organist in a program of ceremony music?

A As with so many other facets of the wedding, referrals are the most reliable source for learning of the best area professionals. Most organists will be happy to suggest musicians they know or have previously worked with. Family members and other married friends may also know of talented musicians.

530

Q What is the appropriate dress code for the musicians that play at the ceremony?

A Assuming that the wedding is a formal affair, the musicians should be dressed in formalwear for the gentlemen, and simple black dresses or white blouses over black skirts for the women.

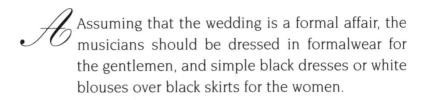

Q What information should the bride-to-be provide the musicians?

A In addition to the date, time, and place of the marriage service, the bride might put the various musicians in touch with each other if they have not previously worked together at a wedding.

∽532∽

Q What details related to the ceremony music should be confirmed in writing with each of the hired musicians?

A A letter of agreement should include the number of musicians, length of time for the performance, number of breaks, the requested dress code, and the price for the performance. A price for any overtime performance should also be noted.

∽533∽

Q Is it acceptable to ask a relative or close friend to perform at the wedding?

A It is thoughtless and potentially embarrassing to allow well-intentioned amateurs the opportunity to perform at the wedding. The couple may relegate such performances for the bridal showers, rehearsal dinner, or reception, while turning to professional musicians to perform at the wedding.

∽534∽

Q How does the location of the ceremony site influence the choice of music for the marriage ceremony?

A In many cases, the setting for the marriage ceremony gives rise to the most compatible type of
wedding music. For example, a soloist singing
Elizabethan love songs accompanied by guitar is
more appropriate at a garden wedding, while a
trumpet fanfare is best suited to a classic church.

∞535∞

Q How does the type of wedding service influence the choice of music for the marriage ceremony?

A Classical music is a suitable complement at most weddings, while acoustical folk or world music is more compatible with specific venues.

∞536∞

Q In what ways can the ceremony music be personalized for a bride and groom?

A When choosing music for the prelude or processional, the bride-to-be might select songs that were favorite tunes at each of their parents' weddings. A brief reference to the meaningfulness of the songs would be a lovely, sentimental touch in the wedding program.

Couples may also enjoy turning to their ethnic heritage for inspiration, opting to include Scottish bagpipes or Jewish klezmer music.

∞537∞

Q What are some of the most popular musical selections for a processional?

Among the favorite processional tunes are "Canon in D" by Pachelbel, "Trumpet Voluntary" by Thomas Dupuis, "Prince of Denmark's March" by Clarke, "Processional of Joy" by Beethoven, "Six Processionals" by Handel, and "Bridal Chorus" by Wagner.

∞538∞

What are some of the most popular musical selections for a recessional?

Among the favorite recessional tunes are "Trumpet Tune" by Purcell, "Hornpipe" by Handel, "Carillon-Sortie" by Mulet, "Sonata Prima" by Vivaldi, "Trumpet Fanfare" by Mouret, and "Wedding March" by Mendelssohn.

∞539∞

How are the finances of hiring the wedding musicians handled?

Once the bride makes her decisions and determines the group's availability on her wedding day, she should simultaneously offer to provide a letter of agreement and a deposit.

↶540↷

Q When is the balance of the musician's fee due?

A The bride-to-be and her family should prepare checks in advance to issue final payment to each of the musicians on the wedding day.

↶541↷

Q What unexpected fees might be incurred by the newlyweds related to the reception music?

A Most musical groups who play at wedding receptions will have a set overtime fee that goes into effect if the newlyweds authorize additional time past the contracted end time.

↶542↷

Q What role does music contribute to a wedding reception?

A The reception music is often considered the pulse of the party and the source for controlling the program of events.

∞543∞

Q What factors help to determine the best music for the wedding reception?

A The top two factors that influence the type of music for the reception are budget and the venue. The music for the reception sets the tone for the celebration of the marriage, and every bride-to-be should work to get the most her money can buy.

⚮544⚮

Q How does the location of the wedding reception affect the choice of music and the musicians?

A The size of the reception site as well as the surroundings determine the proper amount of sound to entertain the guests.

⚮545⚮

Q What are some of the most popular types of musicians for the wedding reception?

A Reception music choices range from a soloist to a string quartet to a large, 24-piece orchestra.

⚮546⚮

Q What factors should be considered when choosing the music for the wedding reception?

A The bride-to-be should ask for the band director's assistance to assure a diverse musical program that appeals to the parents and older guests as well as the newlyweds' friends.

1000 Questions About Your Wedding

1   Introduction

---

1   Your Engagement

---

2   Beginning to Plan

---

3   The Bridal Party

---

4   Wedding Fashions

---

5   Wedding Jewelry/Accessories

---

6   Invitations/Stationery

---

7   Flowers

Music 8

Photography/Videography 9

Bridal Gift Registry 10

The Marriage Ceremony 11

The Wedding Reception 12

Cakes 13

The Honeymoon 14

Your First Home 15

∞547∞

Q What is the most popular complaint by guests at the reception?

A If the music is consistently loud through the entire reception period, the guests will not be able to engage in conversation or enjoy the meal service. Brides should plan a variety of musical formats.

∽548∾

Q How might a bride provide a balanced musical program at the reception?

A With guidance by the band's musical director, the bride should assemble a selection of music to serve as background for the three major segments of the reception. Upbeat songs set a festive tone during the cocktail reception, while a modest number of musicians play a light background of tunes during the meal service. After dinner, the tempo picks up in a wide range of tunes that invite the guests to dance.

∽549∾

Q What is the recommended relationship between the size of the reception musical group and the number of guests?

A There is no set formula for calculating the ratio of musicians and wedding guests since accomplished musicians will adjust their sound level to fit their environment. Nevertheless, the bigger the wedding, the bigger the band.

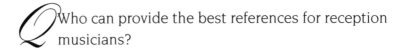

↶550↷

Q Who can provide the best references for reception musicians?

A The bride-to-be should seek the advice of other brides as well as relatives and friends who have attended recent weddings and heard enjoyable reception musicians.

   Wedding consultants and other wedding professionals are another excellent source for recommending good resources.

↶551↷

Q Is it acceptable to drop in on another bride's reception just to hear the band?

A Although any number of musicians will invite a potential couple to hear and see their performance, it is considered bad form to crash someone else's wedding. The couple should look for personal recommendations from trusted sources, listen to audiotapes, or view wedding videos to have a vivid impression of the musical group they are considering.

∞552∞

Q What qualities should a musical group possess in order to be considered as a couple's reception entertainers?

A Among the attributes of the most successful reception musicians are experience in the business, flexibility to provide what the couple want, and knowledge of a broad range of music titles. The couple should request a list of popular reception tunes and cross off any that they prefer not be played at their wedding.

∞553∞

Q What is the most important attribute the reception musicians should possess?

A Rather than hire a group that will take over the reception, a couple should secure musicians who will glide through the events of the program yet not dominate the occasion.

∞554∞

Q What types of music are most popular at wedding receptions?

A Big band, waltzes, swing, oldies, and contemporary songs are the most popular dance tunes at a reception.

❧555❧

Q Is there a rule of thumb about the size of the dance floor at a wedding reception?

A Usually, the dance floor is provided by the reception site, although the bride-to-be should check the size of the dance floor to be sure it is large enough to accommodate the number of invited guests.

❧556❧

Q Is it necessary to feed the musicians who play at the reception?

A If the musicians will be performing for several hours, a savvy bride will provide them with refreshments. It is not necessary that the musicians are offered the same food and drink being presented to the guests.

❧557❧

Q What provisions for the musicians are advisable at an outdoor reception?

A A bride-to-be who is planning an outdoor reception should arrange for a tent or attractive shelter to protect the musicians and their instruments from inclement weather.

↬558↫

Q Is it acceptable to request the bandleader to serve as master of ceremonies at the reception and lead the various events?

A Most bandleaders are happy to introduce the wedding party, announce the first dance and cake cutting, as well as invite the unmarried female guests to join in the bouquet toss.

↬559↫

Q What special events during the reception should have musical accompaniment selected by the bride- and groom-to-be?

A The wedding memories of a lifetime will be etched for the newlyweds against a musical background. Special songs might be played for the couple's first dance, the bride's dance with her father and the groom's dance with his mother, the toasts, cake cutting, bouquet toss, and the newlyweds' departure.

∽560∾

Q What advantages does a professional disc jockey provide in coordinating the music at a wedding reception?

A A good disc jockey will select a range of music—contemporary tunes, oldies, big band, jazz, classical, etc.—to satisfy the tastes of a broad cross section of the wedding guests.

∽561∾

Q Where should a bride-to-be look for references for a disc jockey?

A Friends and family members might recommend a disc jockey who did a great job at a previous wedding they attended. In addition, other wedding professionals like the caterer or photographer may be able to recommend a talented disc jockey.

∽562∾

Q How can a couple determine the best disc jockey for their reception?

Although disc jockeys are rarely auditioned, the couple should arrange a face-to-face meeting to discuss the particulars of their wedding.

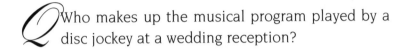

Q Who makes up the musical program played by a disc jockey at a wedding reception?

A An experienced disc jockey should listen to the details of a couple's wedding and then make recommendations about some popular songs that fit the style and mood of the wedding. At the same time, the bride- and groom-to-be should prepare a list of favorite tunes they would enjoy hearing and dancing to at the reception.

If there are certain songs that a bride does not want played at the reception, she should prepare a similar list for the disc jockey.

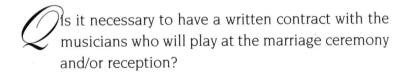

Q Is it necessary to have a written contract with the musicians who will play at the marriage ceremony and/or reception?

A A written contract should spell out all the musical details of the wedding, including the time of arrival, amount of time projected for setup, list of tunes to be played, and overtime fees.

∞565∞

Q Who typically pays for the services of the wedding musicians?

A Traditionally, the bride's family incurs the expenses for the wedding music.

∞566∞

Q What is the typical pricing structure for the wedding musicians?

A In a musical group, each member may need to be paid separately by the hour. Or a nominal fee may be charged for the entire session. The most important key is for the bride to know ahead of time what is involved.

∞567∞

Q What requests related to dress code may the bride-to-be make of all the wedding musicians?

A The bride should specify the style of clothing preferred and confirm the details in her contract.

9

Photography/ Videography

∞568∞

Q Is it advisable to have a friend shoot the wedding photos or video?

A As with every other aspect of the wedding, it's always a smart move to hire a professional to produce the photography. Creation of the memories of a lifetime should not be delegated to a shutterbug friend.

∞569∞

Q How should the wedding photographer or videographer be selected?

A Family members and friends can offer advice about the work of photographers or videographers they've admired. The bridal couple should review the works of several professionals before deciding their preference.

∞570∞

Q What are the two most important points in selecting a photographer and videographer?

A Every bridal couple wants a professional team that offers great images and a good rapport in working closely together.

∞571∞   **9**

Q What subjects should be discussed with the photographer and videographer during the interview process?

A The bridal couple should communicate honestly and clearly with the photographer and videographer about the details of the wedding and share personal facts that distinguish their personal style. There is no such thing as offering too much information at this time.

∞572∞

Q What styles of presentation do photographers use in meeting with brides and grooms?

A The majority of photographers have samples of wedding albums previously prepared for other newlywed couples. A small number of photographers prefer to present their work in a slide show or video.

∽573∾

Q What type of film is used by wedding photographers?

A Most professional wedding photographers use color-negative film.

∽574∾

Q What is sepia-toning?

A Sepia-toning refers to a variation on black-and-white photos produced instead with brown tones that provides an antique appearance in the photographs.

∽575∾

Q What are hand-colored photographs?

A Another variation on traditional black-and-white prints features the process of hand-tinting to add a light touch of color.

∞576∞

Q When should the photographer be booked?

A Since the best photographers tend to be scheduled months in advance, the photographer should be hired early in the planning.

∞577∞

Q What is the process to confirm a photographer?

A After interviewing several photographers to find the best person to capture the wedding on film, enter into a contract that confirms all details and prices.

∞578∞

Q Is a deposit necessary to secure the photographer?

A Virtually all photographers will require a deposit ranging from one-third to one-half of the estimated bill at the time the contract is signed.

ༀ579ༀ

Q How much should a bride and groom expect to pay for their wedding photographs?

A Many photographers offer pricing that starts as low as five hundred dollars, while the more extensive coverage of the wedding can cost up to two thousand dollars or more.

ༀ580ༀ

Q Is it unusual for the photographer to attempt to sell additional services once the contract has been signed?

A A number of photographers might attempt to upgrade the deal with extra services or additional photographs. Although the practice might seem annoying, the bride and groom might benefit from purchasing additional photographs or albums after the wedding if they are pleased with the photographer's work.

ༀ581ༀ

Q What is the advantage of booking a photography package?

Many professional photographers will offer pack-age plans, often segmented by coverage or by the presold album, that provide financial savings.

Q What is a coverage package?

A Some packages are billed by coverage of the wed-ding, meaning that the photographer will agree to take pictures of certain aspects of the wedding. Usually, these packages cover the marriage cere-mony and the reception for a set fee with any extra coverage available for an additional price.

∞583∞

Q How many meetings should the bridal couple have with the photographer?

A It's advisable for the bride to meet with the pho-tographer before the wedding to list all the images she would like for the album and to con-firm the details and schedule of the wedding day. Many photographers want to visit the wedding and reception sites with the bride about a week before the wedding.

∾584∾

Q Is an engagement portrait necessary?

A Many brides-to-be enjoy the opportunity to pose for an engagement photo that captures the excitement of the upcoming wedding.

∾585∾

Q What are the types of engagement photos?

A While the traditional engagement photo pictured the bride alone, more and more couples are choosing a portrait that also includes the groom-to-be.

∾586∾

Q Where should the engagement photo be taken?

A This posed picture is most often taken in the photographer's studio, although the bride-to-be or the couple may opt for an outdoor shot.

∽587∾

Q Should the engagement photo be shot in black-and-white or color?

A The bride-to-be should view a range of samples produced by the photographer to determine her personal preference. If the photo will be published in the newspaper, a black-and-white print should be prepared.

∽588∾

Q What instructions should be given to the photographer before the wedding?

A The bridal couple should decide on the ratio of posed versus candid photographs for the wedding album.

∽589∾

Q How much input should the photographer have in scheduling the events of the wedding day and suggesting the places where these events take place?

A An experienced photographer can offer worthy advice on the timing of events such as the first dance, cake cutting, and bouquet toss.

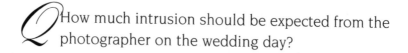

590

Q How much intrusion should be expected from the photographer on the wedding day?

A The photographer might require the use of a flash to capture a range of images, or might need to ask that a pose be held for an extra moment.

591

Q What is the value of candid photography compiled on the wedding day?

A Candid photographs help to balance the posed shots and family portraiture, and document the spontaneous emotion of the wedding party and guests.

592

Q What is photojournalism?

A Photojournalism is a term given to the popular style of candid photography created by the low-profile visions of the photographer.

༺593༻

Q What are photography proofs?

A The photographer will process all of the film taken on the wedding day and produce small prints, known as proofs. They can be made in several sizes, including 3 1/2" x 5", 4" x 6", or 5" x 5".

The wedding proofs may be presented stacked in order of timing or may be arranged in a proof book. Each proof is numbered to facilitate ordering prints for the wedding album.

༺594༻

Q How much time is necessary for the photographer to produce the wedding album?

A Newlyweds can expect to allow up to three months for delivery of the wedding album following the selection of proofs.

༺595༻

Q Is it necessary to order parents' albums?

A A smaller version of the wedding album with special attention to family poses will be a treasured keepsake of both sets of parents. Most likely the price of assembling the parents' albums will be less if it is ordered at the same time as the wedding album.

Q How should the wedding album be compiled?

A The photographer should recreate the story of the wedding day with a collection of scenes that include the setting, the main characters, and the supporting cast caught in the celebration of the day.

597

Q Should all the images in the wedding album be the same size?

A A custom-designed album can arrange large photographs of people with smaller shots of the setting and candid moments for a more interesting effect.

598

Q Can the bride's formal wedding portrait be photographed on the wedding day or should it be shot in advance?

Many brides prefer to have their formal portrait prepared in advance of the wedding day in order to display the framed photograph at their reception. Nevertheless, a formal portrait produced on the wedding day will reflect the unmistakable sparkle of a bride on the day she marries, with her actual hairstyle, makeup, and bouquet.

∞599∞

When should the shooting of the wedding portrait be scheduled?

Schedule the sitting for the wedding portrait about one month prior to the wedding.

∽600∾

Q Where should the wedding portrait be taken?

A Many brides prefer the tradition of a classic photograph shot in the studio, while others have opted to pose in an outdoor setting or at home in a relaxed setting.

∽601∾

Q What details should the bride remember when preparing for her wedding portrait?

A The bride needs to schedule a pressing of her wedding gown by the staff of her bridal salon and arrange for the dress to be returned after the shoot for freshening before the wedding day. The florist should create a silk replica of the bridal bouquet, and a hair and makeup stylist should be booked.

∽602∾

Q Do the bride and her maids require extra makeup for the photography and videography?

A To look their best on both film and tape, the bridal party should apply slightly more makeup than typically worn on a daily basis. A professional beauty stylist can be counted on to apply proper foundation with necessary contours and highlights.

∞603∞

Q Should the groom and groomsmen also wear makeup?

A Many men in the wedding party can benefit from a light application of makeup to enhance their appearance on film and tape.

∞604∞

Q Should the bridal portrait be produced in black-and-white or color?

A The bridal couple should view examples of both styles of portraits produced by their photographer to determine their personal preference. If a copy of the bride's portrait will appear in the newspaper, the photographer should be instructed to provide a black-and-white print.

∞605∞

Q Is it possible to combine black-and-white photos with color photos in the wedding album?

A Many photographers are adept at shooting basic events of the wedding and all the portraiture in color while simultaneously capturing the behind-the-scenes and detail shots in black-and-white. The two sets of pictures can artistically be arranged in the same album.

∞606∞

Q When should the family and wedding party photos be taken?

A Many bridal couples will opt to shoot as many posed pictures as possible before the marriage ceremony in order for the wedding party to arrive promptly at the reception. Some brides believe it is bad luck for the groom to see them before the ceremony, and will make special effort to shoot all the photos not requiring the couple together before the service.

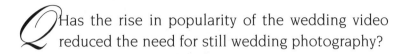

Q Has the rise in popularity of the wedding video reduced the need for still wedding photography?

A Classic wedding photography and videography complement each other. Still prints offer a sense of the moment and record family portraiture for future generations, while video simultaneously captures the activity and sounds at the marriage ceremony and reception.

Q How should the photographer and videographer dress for the wedding?

A All the camera people should dress in the same attire as the guests in order to blend in with the crowd.

Q When interviewing potential videographers, what points should the bridal couple consider?

The videographer should provide existing tapes of previous weddings for review. The bridal couple should view at least one entire tape since poor cameramen sometimes disguise their faults by piecing the best scenes from several weddings to create an overall favorable impression.

A good video picture is sharp, crisp, and in focus, and the cameraman should have a steady hand. A professional videographer smoothly moves from one scene to the next and correctly anticipates what is about to happen. A variety of musical background contributes to the appropriate mood.

∽610∾

Q What steps are involved in booking the photographer and videographer?

A Most photographers and videographers will present a contract for their services and request a deposit to confirm the booking.

∽611∾

Q What are the standard terms of payment for the photographer and videographer?

A Following payment of a deposit at the time the professionals are booked, many couples will be asked to submit an additional payment on the wedding day, with the final payment due upon delivery of the finished wedding album or video.

∞612∞

Q When should the photographer begin shooting on the wedding day?

A Many couples appreciate photographs taken during the hours before the wedding, showing the wedding party dressing and preparations being put into place at the reception site.

∞613∞

Q What should the bride and groom keep in mind in order to look the best in their wedding photos and video?

A Everyone will look best if they are relaxed and act naturally as the images are being recorded.

∞614∞

Q Is it true that the camera tends to add pounds to the images captured on film and tape?

A Since professional photographers and videographers use sophisticated lenses in creating their art, there is no noticeable distortion of body shapes.

∞615∞

Q What should the bride or groom who wears eyeglasses keep in mind on the wedding day?

A Brides- and grooms-to-be who wear glasses at all times should inform their photographer of the fact as they confirm the booking. The photographer will be careful to offer instructions about posing that should avoid glare and reflections from the eyeglasses.

∞616∞

Q What are the rules about shooting photographs with a flash during the marriage ceremony?

Many houses of worship forbid the use of flash photography. The wedding director at the church or synagogue can provide specific information.

∞617∞

Q How can couples restrict the use of cameras by family members and friends at the wedding?

A Both the bride's family and groom's family should employ word of mouth to request that guests do not bring cameras to the marriage ceremony. Well-intentioned shutterbug family members and friends may indeed disturb the professional photographer's coverage of the ceremony as well as distract other guests.

Amateur shutterbugs may not pose as much of a problem at the reception, although they should be cautioned to restrain from taking pictures while the photographer is shooting.

∞618∞

Q Should single-use cameras be provided at the reception?

A Many couples are distributing single-use cameras for the guests to shoot a montage of candid pictures throughout the hours of the reception. The cameras are typically collected at the end of the party and processed by the bride's family or the newlyweds. Shutterbug friends will usually produce great quality photos and manage to capture spontaneous views missed by the professional photographer.

619

Q Should table shots at the reception be part of the wedding album?

A Many couples will request the photographer to shoot group shots by table at the reception to assure that all guests are included in the wedding album.

620

Q How should the guests be positioned in a table shot?

A Rather than simply approaching the table and framing all the guests in their seats, the photographer should ask half the guests at the table to stand behind the seated guests. With such a pose, the photographer can focus on the faces of the guests without sacrificing significant space to the table surface.

∞621∞

Q How early should the videographer arrive before the wedding?

A The videographer should arrive a few hours before the taping begins to become familiar with the setup and meet all the important people.

∞622∞

Q What should the bridal couple prepare for the photographer and videographer before the wedding?

A A list of main events should be provided to both to ensure that neither misses a crucial moment.

∞623∞

Q What factors affect the price of a wedding video?

A Pricing is dictated by the amount of time covered by tape coupled with the amount of editing required to produce the finished tape.

∞624∞

Q What are the types of shots featured in a wedding video?

A Long shots are the long-distance views that provide a sense of the setting, medium shots are closer views, and close-ups focus on specific details.

∞625∞

Q What importance is pacing in a wedding video?

A Pacing, or the compilation of long, medium, and close-up views, is essential to the creation of an enjoyable wedding video.

∞626∞

Q What is the advantage of including prewedding video in the bridal video?

A Many videographers have found artistic ways to show the couple in a relaxed setting during their engagement as a lead-in to the wedding day video. Participating in this project may help the couple and the videographer get to know each other and become more relaxed about working together on the wedding day.

⚮627⚮

Q How many cameramen should cover a wedding?

A The majority of weddings are adequately covered by one cameraman with a few assistants.

⚮628⚮

Q How long should a wedding video be?

A The length of the video is dictated by the amount and depth of details documented on tape, although most couples opt for an hour-long video.

⚮629⚮

Q How intrusive should a videographer be at a wedding?

A While most video equipment is sensitive to the limited light available in many wedding settings, some videographers will determine it necessary to supplement the natural setting with the occasional use of extra light.

❧630❧

Q What is a video interview?

A A growing trend in wedding videos today is the inclusion of messages and best wishes from the guests of the wedding. The bridal couple should request the videographer to instruct each participant to introduce himself or herself and keep comments brief.

❧631❧

Q Is it possible to use copyrighted music on a wedding video?

A The music industry has allowed the use of favorite songs to accompany videos for private use without requiring conventional patent fees.

❧632❧

Q What is dubbing?

A Dubbing refers to the copying of a video.

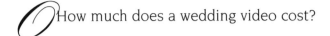

633

Q How much does a wedding video cost?

A Prices can range broadly from two hundred dollars for the simplest tape produced with no editing to twelve hundred dollars or more for a highly edited version that features the work of several cameramen.

634

Q What should couples with stepparents or divorced parents consider in designing their wedding photography?

A Diplomacy may be necessary in keeping the extended family stress-free during the wedding, especially as the wedding pictures are taken. The bride-to-be and her fiancé should have frank conversations with everyone before the wedding as a means of smoothing tensions and making plans for the compilation of family photos for the wedding album.

635

Q In addition to the ceremony and reception, what other occasions might warrant the presence of a professional photographer or videographer?

A Many wedding celebrations feature a series of parties—bridesmaids' luncheon, rehearsal dinner, going-away brunch—that can be captured by film or tape.

636

Q What special provisions should the bride-to-be arrange for the photography and videography crews?

A Since everyone helping to create the wedding album and video will be working many hours, it's a good idea to order food service for them during the event. The crew may be seated at a separate table from the guests or offered a comfortable, behind-the-scenes area to relax briefly.

637

Q Should the photographer or videographer receive a tip?

A Photographers and videographers are profession-als who bill for their services and don't expect an additional tip. Each should receive a thank-you note from the bride, and extra-special service might be accompanied with a gift as a token of appreciation.

10

Bridal Gift Registry

∽638∽

Q. What is the bridal gift registry?

A growing number of department and specialty stores offer a complimentary service of listing an engaged couple's wedding gift preferences.

∽639∽

What is the purpose of the bridal gift registry service?

For engaged couples, a bridal gift registry service provides an opportunity to identify the items that they would enjoy receiving as gifts for their new home.

∽640∽

Is it considered in good taste for an engaged couple to promote such a list of desired gifts?

Although traditional etiquette recommends that it is otherwise not proper to announce gift preferences, modern times have embraced the bridal gift registry as a practical service for guests to choose gift items that a couple want and need.

∞641∞

Q How soon should a couple establish their gift registry list?

A Couples may create their gift list as soon as they
become engaged and set the wedding date. The
advantage of setting up a list early is for family
members and friends to utilize the list in choosing
engagement and shower gifts.

10

∞642∞

Q How is the gift registry list managed?

A While some smaller, specialty retailers operate
with a manually maintained list of the couple's
gift preferences, a majority of stores offer consumers a self-service, computer-operated system
for accessing the gift list.

∞643∞

Q How is the couple's gift list maintained?

A As family members and friends access the couple's
registry list and purchase items for them, the computer removes those selections and maintains a

current roster of the desired products to avoid duplicate gift-giving.

∞644∞

Q What is the procedure for a couple to list their gift preferences with a retailer?

A Because the retailer will want to offer personal service to each couple, most stores recommend that a couple arrange an appointment with a bridal registry consultant to create their list.

∞645∞

Q How should a couple prepare for their initial meeting with the bridal registry consultant?

A Couples should study the pages of **Elegant Bride** to determine their taste preferences as well as browse through the store selection to identify products and patterns they admire.

∞646∞

Q How much time should a couple allow for the initial meeting with the bridal registry consultant?

Most retailers schedule about one hour for the initial meeting.

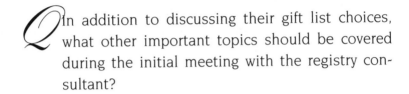

647

 In addition to discussing their gift list choices, what other important topics should be covered during the initial meeting with the registry consultant?

Each retailer will observe its own systems and policies regarding the creation of a couple's wish list and the future return or exchange of gifts. It's a good idea to review these policies at the very beginning in order to eliminate unnecessary confusion later.

648

What products should be included on the gift registry list?

The basic categories of gift choices include tableware; bed, bath, and table linens; cookware and appliances; and furniture and decorative accessories.

649

Q How can a couple be sure to receive the exact item they prefer?

A In listing the items for the gift registry, the couple should provide complete product information, including manufacturer, model number, color, and quantity needed.

650

Q What basic table-setting rule should a couple observe when choosing their china, crystal, and silver patterns?

A A good rule of thumb that assures an interesting combination of china, crystal, and silver is the "two to one" principle. This simple dictum suggests that a table setting include two plain elements with one fancy element or two fancy elements with one plain element. In other words, a decorated china pattern and ornate silver pattern would be best balanced with a simply styled crystal pattern; a classic, banded china pattern and a sleek crystal stem would be best matched with a detailed silver pattern.

∞651∞

Q Is it necessary to register for two different table-ware services, one for formal occasions and one for every day?

A Many couples appreciate the opportunity to acquire all the tableware items they can possibly use by choosing separate, yet complete sets of tableware in formal as well as casual themes on their bridal registry. Knowing that family members and friends are anxious to assist them in setting up their first home, these couples often choose classic, timeless patterns of formal china, crystal, and silver that will be used primarily on very special occasions–holidays and anniversaries–during the early years of marriage and serve as the foundation of their entertaining style in years to come. At the same time, these couples choose a favorite pattern that they stack in the kitchen cabinets to use every day.

∞652∞

Q How can a couple maximize the use of their fine tableware with mix-and-match patterns?

A As a means of projecting their own personal style, more and more couples are coordinating a variety of tableware patterns to achieve a unique look. The easiest addition is a selection of decorative salad/dessert plates chosen to coordinate with a simple, banded china pattern. In addition, stylish couples are mixing and matching their crystal stemware as well, choosing coordinating stems from different patterns that have an appealing look when placed together.

⟳653⟲

Q What factors should a couple consider when choosing their china patterns?

A Most couples pay attention to the color of their decorating scheme as well as their preferred design style.

⟳654⟲

Q What are the most popular design styles of china?

A The four basic design categories include banded, floral, geometric, and Oriental.

∞655∞

Q What is the difference between porcelain and bone china?

A Porcelain is made from kaolin (white china clay), quartz, and feldspar that is fired at extremely high temperatures to become glassy and nonporous. Bone china is made from porcelain with the addition of bone ash, producing a whiter, more translucent tableware.

∞656∞

Q Can fine china be used in the oven?

A The majority of gold-accented china pieces cannot withstand use in an oven, and couples should check the product label for instructions on microwave- and oven-proof usage.

∞657∞

Q Can fine china be cleaned in the dishwasher?

A Most gold decoration and hand-painted details may become damaged by the cleaning cycles of the dishwasher, and most manufacturers advise gentle hand washing of better tableware.

658

Q What pieces make up a place setting of fine china?

A Fine china is usually available in five-piece place settings, including a dinner plate, salad plate, bread-and-butter plate, cup, and saucer.

659

Q For how many place settings should a couple register?

A Most couples register for at least eight place settings of fine china, and usually request twelve place settings with matching serving accessories.

660

Q What serving accessories are typically available to match a place setting?

A In addition to the place setting, most china patterns also include several platters, a vegetable bowl, covered casserole, salt and pepper shakers, sugar bowl and creamer, coffeepot or teapot, and gravy boat plus mugs, soup/cereal bowls, and fruit bowls.

∞661∞

Q What is the difference between earthenware and stoneware?

A Earthenware is made of clay and is typically heavy in scale and yet available in a wide range of colors. Known for its tendency to crack and chip, earthenware is priced in the low-to-middle retail price points.

Stoneware is made from a combination of clay and feldspar that when fired at high temperatures produces a heavy dinnerware with the hardness of stone.

∞662∞

Q What pieces are typically offered in a casual dinnerware place setting?

A Most casual dinnerware patterns offer a four-piece place setting, including dinner plate, salad plate, soup/cereal bowl, and mug.

∞663∞

Q For how many place settings of casual dinnerware should a couple register?

A Since many casual dinnerware patterns are packaged with four place settings to a box, most couples request either eight or twelve place settings.

∞664∞

Q What factors should a couple consider when choosing their crystal stemware?

A Most couples consider the type of decoration on the body of the stem, including cuts and etchings, the availability of gold accent, and the basic shape of the bowl of the stem.

∞665∞

Q What are the basic stems in a place setting of crystal?

A Most couples automatically register for wineglasses, water goblets, and champagne flutes. Depending upon the pattern, the couple may have the choice of red or white wineglasses, or champagne flutes or coupes. In addition to their obvious purpose, each stem can doubly serve alternative beverages or foods, including juice or iced tea in the water goblet, and fresh fruit, sorbet, or ice cream in the champagne flute.

666

Q For how many place settings of fine crystal should a couple register?

A Couples typically register for the same number of china and crystal place settings, usually requesting twelve place settings of each.

667

Q For what other crystal barware pieces should a couple register?

A In addition to the basic place setting, most couples add cordial and iced-beverage glasses, highballs, and double old-fashioned glasses.

668

Q Is it acceptable for a couple to choose a separate crystal pattern for their barware, or should the pattern match their stemware?

Since barware is typically used before guests are seated for dinner, it is perfectly acceptable to choose a different pattern for barware, which is often more casual in style than the formal stemware.

∽669∾

Q Can crystal stemware be cleaned in the dishwasher?

A Many fine crystal pieces can be cleaned in the dishwasher, provided they are securely placed with ample space between the stems. Most brides feel more comfortable washing their fine crystal by hand, adding a splash of household ammonia to help maintain the sparkle and a touch of vinegar in the rinse water to prevent spotting.

∽670∾

Q What factors should a couple consider in choosing their silver flatware?

A The basic design styles of flatware are traditional or contemporary and ornate or refined. Another decision is the grade of flatware, including sterling silver, silverplate, or stainless steel.

❦671❦

Q What is the difference between sterling silver and silverplate?

A Sterling silver is the finest and most expensive quality of silver, composed of 92.5 percent pure silver and 7.5 percent of a strengthening alloy, usually copper. Silverplate, on the other hand, consists of a layer of silver over some other base metal.

❦672❦

Q What is stainless steel flatware made from?

A Stainless steel flatware is composed from a mixture of steel, chromium, and nickel. It is considered the most durable flatware for regular use.

❦673❦

Q What pieces are included in the basic five-piece place setting of flatware?

A A five-piece place setting includes a dinner fork, dinner knife, salad or dessert fork, dessert or soup spoon, and a teaspoon.

∞674∞

Q: What pieces are included in a four-piece place setting of flatware?

A: A four-piece place setting includes a dinner fork, dinner knife, salad or dessert fork, and teaspoon.

∞675∞

Q: What pieces are included in a six-piece place setting of flatware?

A: A six-piece place setting includes a dinner fork, dinner knife, salad or dessert fork, dessert or soup spoon, teaspoon, and butter spreader.

∞676∞

Q: How is everyday stainless steel flatware sold?

A: Although most stainless steel patterns are available in single place settings, they are often packaged in sets of four, eight, or twelve place settings.

∞677∞

Q For how many place settings of silver flatware should a couple register?

A It is best to register for twelve place settings, in keeping with the same number of requested china and crystal place settings.

∞678∞

Q Besides the basic place setting, what additional silver flatware pieces are usually available in each pattern?

A Additional silver flatware items include iced-beverage spoons, serving spoons and forks plus a pierced serving spoon, gravy ladle, pastry server, and sugar spoon.

∞679∞

Q Relative to sterling flatware, what is the patina?

A The patina is the gleaming finish produced by the frequent use of sterling silver flatware.

∞680∞

Q Is it necessary to polish fine silver?

A Even silver that is regularly used and has a lustrous patina will need an occasional polish with a cream-style cleaner.

∞681∞

Q Can silver flatware be cleaned in the dishwasher?

A Although many silver patterns are dishwasher-safe, most brides prefer to wash their sterling by hand in hot water with a mild detergent and dry with a soft, cotton cloth. Carved details can be cleaned with a soft-bristle brush.

∞682∞

Q In addition to the basic place settings of china, crystal, and silver, what other serving items should be included on the registry list?

A Many brides prefer to use serveware made of silver, crystal, brass, or wood. Additional items essential to a couple's registry list include trays, bowls, a bread basket, pitcher, and salad bowl. Optional items include a bonbon/butter dish, compote, and tureen.

683

Q What other decorative items should be included on the registry list?

A Most couples will enjoy using picture frames, candlesticks, and vases in a variety of materials throughout their new home.

684

Q What factors should a couple consider when choosing their cookware?

A Depending upon their passion for cooking, newlyweds will appreciate a selection of the basic saucepans and skillets, along with specialty items, to create their favorite dishes. In addition to style and color, cookware is most importantly available in a variety of materials that satisfy a variety of different types of cooking styles and needs.

685

Q What is the advantage of aluminum cookware?

A Aluminum cookware is known for fast, uniform heating and may be available with a nonstick finish for easy cleaning.

686

Q What is anodized cookware?

A Aluminum cookware that is processed in a chemical bath to make it even more durable is known as anodized. It will not react with certain foods and may be available with a nonstick finish for easy cleaning.

687

Q What is the advantage of copper cookware?

A One of the oldest cooking materials, copper cookware is known for providing rapid, even heat. Most copper pans are lined with stainless steel or tin to prevent reactions with acidic foods.

Q What is the advantage of stainless steel cookware?

A Stainless steel pans are often considered the
most durable, and are typically dent-, stain-,
and scratch-resistant. Many stainless steel pans
are available with a layer of copper or aluminum
in the base to provide even heat distribution
while cooking.

Q What is the advantage of enamel-coated stainless
steel cookware?

A The decorative styling of enamel-coated cookware
adds a color and design element to very durable
cookware.

Q What are the advantages of nonstick coatings on
the interior of cookware?

Besides making the clean-up process easier, nonstick finishes allow a cook to use less oils and fats in meal preparation for a more health-conscious diet.

❧691❧

What basic saucepans should be included on the registry list?

Saucepans are typically available in various sizes from one quart up to four quart. A one-quart pan is handy for heating a small amount of food or making sauces. Larger saucepans are suited to steaming vegetables and cooking soup or pasta. At least two sizes of saucepans are essential to any kitchen.

❧692❧

What basic skillets should be included on the registry list?

Skillets range in size from eight inch to twelve inch, and a couple should choose at least two sizes for their registry.

❧693❧

Q What other basic cookware should be included on the registry list?

A A Dutch oven is perfect for preparing stews or casseroles. A larger stock pot allows for cooking in quantity and a roasting pan is perfect for cooking meats. A tea kettle that matches the cookware or coordinates with the kitchen decor is a must for every home.

❧694❧

Q What types of specialty pans are available for preparing certain foods and dishes?

A Couples who enjoy a variety of foods will appreciate registering for a wok, grill pan, omelet pan, soufflé pan, and double boiler.

❧695❧

Q What are the basic pans for baking?

A Essential baking pans include pie and cake pans, cookie sheets, muffin tins, and bread pans.

696

Q What types of cooking utensils should be included on the registry list?

A Although some manufacturers offer sets of cooking utensils, no kitchen should be lacking a variety of large spoons, including a slotted spoon, spatula, ladle, and whisk.

697

Q What are the basic knives needed to equip a kitchen?

A Basic cutlery for the gift registry list should include a paring knife for cutting small foods, a medium-sized utility knife, a chef's knife for cutting larger foods, a carving knife for cutting meats and large vegetables, a bread knife, and a serrated utility knife for slicing tomatoes and juicy items.

698

Q What factors should a couple consider when selecting knives for the bridal registry list?

A Sharp knives are essential to success in food preparation, and any chef would recommend that newlyweds obtain the highest quality cutting utensils. There are three different types of cutting blades to choose from, and couples should also inspect construction details.

∞699∞

Q What are the most popular types of cutting blades?

A Probably the best investment is in high-carbon stainless steel knives that are a combination of sturdy steel with easy-sharpening carbon. However, carbon steel may discolor foods and can chip. Stainless steel knives are the most durable and least expensive, but are difficult to sharpen.

∞700∞

Q What are the most popular small electrical appliances?

A A couple should consider myriad appliances designed to make cooking fun and easy, including a coffeemaker, espresso/cappuccino maker, coffee grinder, toaster or toaster oven, mixer, can opener, juicer, food processor, blender, waffle iron, slow cooker, bread maker, and ice cream maker.

∞701∞

Q What kitchen accessories should be included on the bridal gift registry?

A Decorative yet functional kitchen accessories include a canister set, bread box, spice set, clock, and cutting board.

∞702∞

Q What linens should be selected for the kitchen?

A A selection of terry and linen dish towels should be matched with a range of pot holders and oven mitts.

∞703∞

Q What are the essential gadgets needed to stock a kitchen?

A Some helpful gadgets include a can opener, vegetable peeler, garlic press, cooking shears, measuring cups, pepper mill, nutcracker, apple corer, cheese grater, shrimp deveiner, salad spinner, strainer, colander, timer, flour sifter, rolling pin, and cooling racks.

∽704∾

Q What factors should a couple consider when choosing linens for their master suite?

A The softness of sheets and bedding is determined by fiber content and thread count. In addition, the couple should determine whether the location of their home will require a seasonal change of linens for warm and cool weather.

∽705∾

Q What are the most popular fibers for bed linens?

A Most couples prefer the softness of 100 percent cotton sheeting, which becomes even softer the more often it's used and laundered, while others enjoy luxuriating in silk bedding. A blend of cotton and polyester provides a wrinkle-free sheet that is typically less expensive.

❧ 706 ❧

Q What are the pieces of a fully accessorized bed in the master suite?

A Besides sheets and pillowcases, a dressed bed features a bedspread or comforter with dust ruffle, shams, and several decorative pillows. The couple may also choose to coordinate the window treatments and a table round with their bed linens.

❧ 707 ❧

Q What is a duvet?

A A duvet is essentially a utilitarian comforter stuffed with a variety of fillers that is dressed with a decorative duvet cover. The advantage to having a duvet is that the decorating scheme can be easily changed with a new, relatively inexpensive duvet cover.

❧ 708 ❧

Q What are the most popular materials used to fill comforters and duvets?

A Goose down feathers are the softest, most luxurious filler material that maintains a sumptuous loft without lumping or shifting. Silk fillers offer warmth with very light weight. Man-made fibers are ideal for preventing sensitive allergic reactions that some people may get from goose down fillers.

∞709∞

Q What are the most popular materials for blankets?

A Natural fibers are the most popular for blankets, ranging from cashmere and mohair to merino wool and lighter-weight cotton.

∞710∞

Q What basic furnishings are necessary to protect the bedding?

A Every bed should have a mattress pad under the fitted sheet and a pillow protector under the pillowcase.

∽711∽

Q What is included in a sheet set?

A A number of domestics manufacturers have packaged together all the linens required to make a bed, including a flat sheet, fitted sheet, and two pillowcases.

∽712∽

Q How many towels should be included on the gift registry list?

A Many couples will appreciate having at least six sets of bath linens, including a bath towel, hand towel, and washcloth. Other essentials are a tubmat with coordinating shower curtain, accessories, and bath rug.

In addition, couples who expect to furnish a guest bath should request additional sets of towels for the bath plus linen hand towels. Many couples enjoy adding their monogram to their guest towels.

∽713∽

Q What are the two basic styles of bath towels?

Thick, looped terry towels absorb water quickly while sheared terry towels offer a soft, velvety touch.

❧714❧

Q What is a bath sheet?

A A bath sheet is an oversized bath towel that is at home in the master bath as well as taken to the beach or pool.

❧715❧

Q How many sets of linens should be listed on the bridal gift registry?

A A good rule of thumb is to have three sets of bed linens: one on the bed, one in the linen closet, and one in the laundry.

❧716❧

Q How does a couple choose table linens to complement their tableware?

A Experimenting by putting an actual place mat or napkins with the place setting will quickly identify pretty table linens to match the dinnerware, stemware, and flatware. It's a good idea to select at least two different sets of linens for both the formal and casual tableware in order to create a variety of looks that can be tailored to the entertaining occasion.

∽717∾

Q What additional items may a couple list on their bridal registry?

A Most retailers are interested in helping a newly-wed couple furnish and decorate their entire home, and offer furniture, lamps, floor coverings, and decorative accessories to be added to the couple's registry.

∽718∾

Q Once a couple create their gift list with a retailer, can changes be made to the list?

A Each couple should be easily able to expand to their list as they identify additional products needed for their new home.

∞719∞

Q At how many stores should an engaged couple list their gift choices?

A Although the original concept of the bridal gift registry service recommended that a couple register in just one department store, a growing number of couples are registering at several stores in order to fully outfit their new home.

∞720∞

Q How do the bride and groom inform their guests where they've registered for wedding gifts?

A News of the bridal gift list is information that is only distributed by word of mouth. The couple's mothers as well as the wedding party may share the location of the bridal registry when asked by guests, but the information may not be enclosed with the wedding invitation.

∞721∞

Q Is it permissible for the hostess of a bridal shower to include the location of the couple's bridal registry with the shower invitations?

A The shower invitation is the only document that may include actual notation of the couple's registry.

⚭722⚭

Q Who may host a bridal shower?

A A bridal shower is a party given in honor of the bride-to-be or, as is growing in popularity, the engaged couple. Traditional etiquette dictates that no member of the bride or groom's immediate family host such an event, a move that appears in poor taste as a blatant request for a gift.

Bridal showers should be hosted by friends of the parents, friends of the couple, or the friend's parents.

⚭723⚭

Q What are some popular themes for bridal showers?

A A shower where the engaged couple are the center of attention is a growing trend that involves male and female relatives and friends. Sometimes the hostess may choose a certain room as the focus of the shower–for example, the linens shower where guests select sheets, blankets, and comforters, plus towels for the master suite.

∞724∞

Q Who should be invited to the bridal showers?

A Each guest of a bridal shower should be among the guests invited to the wedding. All guests at the wedding, however, should not necessarily receive an invitation to a shower.

∞725∞

Q How should couples handle the receipt of duplicate wedding gifts?

A Couples can usually easily exchange duplicate gifts for outstanding gifts on their registry. After the wedding, the couple should make an appointment with their bridal registry consultant to expedite their gift exchanges.

The couple should write a thank-you note for the gift to the wedding guest without indicating that it was a duplicate.

726

Q How should couples handle the receipt of damaged products?

A The couple should return the broken gift along with its packaging to the original store and request replacement. A thank-you note should be sent for the gift without indication of the defect.

727

Q How should couples handle the receipt of incomplete sets of products from their gift registry list?

A After the wedding, a couple can opt to purchase the missing pieces with money received at the wedding or to return the incomplete pieces in exchange for other products. Many stores maintain a couple's gift registry list for a year after the wedding, allowing family members and friends an opportunity to purchase requested items for birthday or other holiday gifts.

The
Marriage
Ceremony

☙728☙

Q What is the first step an engaged couple should take in planning their marriage ceremony?

A The engaged couple should meet with their clergyperson or judge to learn the religious and legal requirements that must be fulfilled prior to the wedding. In addition, the couple should inquire about policies of the church or synagogue.

☙729☙

Q What factors should be considered in selecting the location for the marriage ceremony?

A Among the considerations are date availability; seating capacity; rules regarding decorations, music, and photography; and usage and security fees.

☙730☙

Q What facilities are necessary at the marriage ceremony site?

A In order for guests to enjoy the ceremony, the site should be checked for air-conditioning or heating and optimal acoustics.

Most bridal parties also appreciate separate dressing rooms for the bride and her maids and the groomsmen.

11

∞731∞

Q What fees might be incurred in staging the wedding at a house of worship?

A The church or synagogue may impose a usage fee for weddings taking place on its premises or may require that a custodian be on hand to make sure the facilities are in complete working order. Usage fees may be waived for members of the congregation.

In some houses of worship, it may be expected that the bride's family make a donation in honor of the newlyweds as a token of appreciation for the clergyperson's participation.

∞732∞

Q What fees might be incurred in staging the wedding at a neutral site?

A In addition to a usage fee, a neutral site may require payment of a security deposit for extra insurance.

∞733∞

Q How can a couple personalize their marriage ceremony?

A The couple should review the service with their clergyperson at least several weeks before the wedding to determine the rites that can be personalized. Some couples choose to write their own vows, while others choose special readings to incorporate in the service or cultural elements that reflect their heritage.

Special tokens can be distributed to guests at the ceremony, including flowers and a wedding program.

∞734∞

Q How can a special relative or friend be involved in the ceremony?

A Special friends and relatives can present a favorite reading, hymn, or song in the service.

If the guest register is placed at the ceremony site, a relative or friend may be asked to preside over the guestbook.

∞735∞

Q What provisions should be made to transport the wedding party to the ceremony site?

A A traditional stretch limousine can certainly provide enough room for the bride in her gown and her attendants. Other choices include an antique car, trolley, or horse and carriage.

❦736❧

Q What is the traditional order of service for the marriage ceremony?

A Most weddings begin with the prelude and follow with the processional, welcome, readings, benediction, vows, exchange of rings, blessing, and recessional.

❦737❧

Q How long is the average marriage ceremony?

A On average, the marriage ceremony takes about thirty minutes.

❦738❧

Q Is it acceptable to invite guests to the wedding but not the reception?

A It is expected that guests invited to the marriage ceremony will be included at the reception.

⌘739⌘

Q Is it acceptable to invite guests only to the reception?

A In cases where the ceremony site can only accommodate a limited number of guests, or in personal circumstances where the ceremony will be attended only by immediate family members and very close friends, it is permissible to invite guests to celebrate the marriage at the wedding reception.

⌘740⌘

Q How soon before the ceremony begins should the ushers be gathered to welcome guests?

A Although few guests will arrive more than thirty minutes before the service, the ushers should be prepared to greet guests about an hour before the ceremony.

⌘741⌘

Q On what sides of the church are guests seated for a Christian wedding?

A The bride's family and friends are seated on the left side of the church, and the groom's family and friends are seated on the right side.

❧742❧

Q On what side of the synagogue are guests seated for a Jewish wedding?

A The bride's family and friends are seated on the right side of the synagogue, and the groom's family and friends are seated on the left.

❧743❧

Q At what point should the prelude music begin?

A Prelude music to welcome guests should start about thirty minutes before the ceremony.

❧744❧

Q How long should the prelude music last?

A The prelude music should be performed until the processional is ready. If the bride is running behind schedule, the prelude music should continue until all members of the wedding party have assembled.

745

Q How does the processional begin?

A The seating of the grandparents and the mothers is a signal to the guests that the processional is about to begin. The groom's mother should be seated first.

746

Q What happens after the mother of the bride is seated?

A Once both mothers have taken their places, the ushers should unfurl the aisle runner.

747

Q At what point does the clergyperson take his place?

A The clergyperson takes his place just before the processional music begins.

❧748❧

Q When do the groom and the best man take their places?

A The bride has two choices related to the assembly of the men of the wedding party. The men can follow the clergyman before the processional begins, entering from the chancery. In a more formal mode, the processional can begin with the entrance of the ushers, followed by the best man and the groom.

❧749❧

Q How do the bride's attendants take their places?

A The bridesmaids lead the processional, followed by the maid or matron of honor.

❧750❧

Q At what point do the child attendants take their places?

A The children follow the bride's honor attendant, just before the bride.

∞751∞

Q Is it advisable for the ring bearer to carry the wedding bands on his decorative pillow?

A It is the responsibility of the maid or matron of honor and the best man to present the wedding bands for the exchange of rings. It's a good idea for the honor attendants to carry the actual rings and for the ring bearer to have artificial rings attached to his pillow.

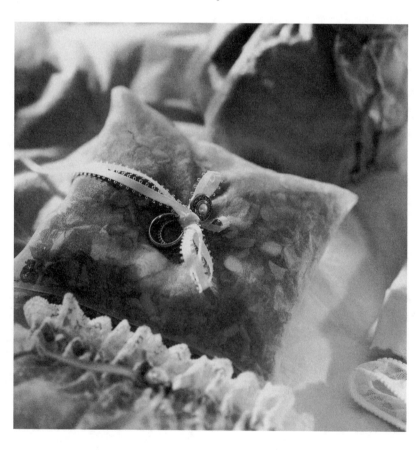

∞752∞

Q Should the ushers and bridesmaids enter in single or double file?

A The bride can determine her preference for the attendants entering singly or in pairs, taking into consideration the number of attendants and the layout of the church or synagogue.

∞753∞

Q At what point does the bride enter the church or synagogue?

A Each member of the wedding party should be in his or her place before the bridal march begins.

∞754∞

Q Is it appropriate for the congregation to stand for the bride's processional?

A The guests should take their cue from the mother of the bride, and stand only if she does.

∽755∾

Q Where should the bridesmaids and groomsmen stand during the marriage ceremony?

A If the altar is large enough to accommodate the entire wedding party, they should stand on either side of the bride and groom.

If the altar cannot hold the wedding party comfortably, the attendants should be seated in the first row of the church or synagogue.

∽756∾

Q How should the bridesmaids and groomsmen be arranged on the altar?

A It is the bride's preference whether the maids and ushers take respective sides of the altar or stand in pairs on either side of the bride and groom.

∽757∾

Q Who traditionally escorts the bride down the aisle?

A The bride's father typically takes the honor of escorting his daughter down the aisle.

∽758∾

Q If the bride's father is deceased, who escorts her down the aisle?

A A grandfather, brother, uncle, or close male friend may escort her down the aisle.

∽759∾

Q Is it proper for the bride to proceed down the aisle without an escort?

A It is not mandatory that the bride have an escort for the march down the aisle. Older brides, in particular, may choose to walk down the aisle alone.

∽760∾

Q If the bride's parents were divorced when she was very young, she may have had limited contact with her real father and feels closer to her stepfather. Who should walk her down the aisle?

A Only the bride can decide which man will have the honor of escorting her down the aisle, but it appears that a stronger bond with the stepfather should give him the privilege. She should try to recognize her father in a special way on the wedding day, perhaps asking him to give a reading during the ceremony or with a dance at the reception.

∽761∾

Q How can a couple of different faiths blend each denomination in the marriage ceremony?

A Many interfaith couples will invite each of their clergypersons to share in conducting the wedding service. Every religion has traditions that can be incorporated into the ceremony.

∽762∾

Q What is the "jumping the broom" tradition that can be incorporated in the marriage ceremony?

A Traditional African-American brides choose to blend a cultural element into their contemporary marriage ceremony by reenacting a legacy that dates back to the era of slavery. In the colonial days, slaves were not allowed the privilege of a formal marriage, but those who were spiritual created their own tradition whereby they gathered family and friends to offer thanks and ask for God's blessing. At the conclusion of the ceremony, the couple literally jumped over a broom to symbolize their step into matrimony.

❧763❧

Q What is the order of the processional in a Jewish wedding?

A The rabbi and cantor lead the Jewish processional, followed by the grandparents, the ushers, the groom escorted by his parents, the bridesmaids, and the bride escorted by her parents.

❧764❧

Q What is the symbolism of the chuppah used in Jewish weddings?

A The chuppah, or wedding canopy, which is a representation of the Jewish home, offers shelter and yet remains open to the world. This sanctuary without walls is erected on the altar, under which the wedding party stands during the marriage service.

❧765❧

Q What is the symbolism of the ketubah in the Jewish wedding service?

A The ketubah, or wedding covenant, is a marriage contract signed by the bride and groom in front of witnesses before the ceremony. The ancient ketubah protected the bride's rights as a married woman and assured her care and protection by the groom.

∞766∞

Q What is the symbolism of the aufruf held during the Sabbath morning service preceding the wedding?

A The aufruf, a German word meaning "calling up," refers to the rite at which the prospective bride and groom join the rabbi on the bimah (pulpit) to participate in the Torah reading. It is traditional for the rabbi to share some personal remarks about the upcoming wedding and offer a blessing for the couple's happiness. Sometimes, as the bride- and groom-to-be return to their seats, the congregation showers them with candy as a symbol of their good wishes for a sweet and fulfilling marriage.

∞767∞

Q What is the symbolism of breaking the glass at the conclusion of the Jewish wedding ceremony?

A Following the rabbi's pronouncing the couple as husband and wife, the groom stomps on glass wrapped in a linen napkin. The shattered glass serves as a reminder of the destruction of the Temple in Jerusalem, teaches that even in times of great joy there is also sadness in life, and warns that love, like glass, is fragile and must be protected.

∽768∾

Q What information should be included in the wedding program?

A The wedding program should list the order of service and the musical accompaniments along with the members of the wedding party. Some couples take the opportunity to express their personal thoughts of thanks and love for their family and friends.

∽769∾

Q What is the tradition of the unity candle?

A The unity candle symbolizes the joining of two families and is lit by the bridal couple after professing their vows. Typically, a small station is arranged near the altar containing two tapered candles and a larger, decorated unity candle.

As each mother is escorted to her seat before the processional, she approaches the station and lights a candle to represent her family. The individual candles burn throughout the service until the newlyweds take their respective candles and together ignite the unity candle.

∽770∼

Q When should a rehearsal of the marriage ceremony be scheduled?

A Most rehearsals take place the day before the wedding, and may be followed by a rehearsal dinner celebration. The rehearsal should be scheduled at a time when all members of the wedding party can be in attendance.

∽771∼

Q Who is authorized to preside over a civil ceremony?

A Regulations vary by state, and officiants in addition to the clergy may include a judge, the justice of the peace, the mayor, or a county clerk.

❧772❧

Q If the wedding will be a civil ceremony, where can the service take place?

A A civil ceremony can be staged in any number of locations, including at home, in a garden, at poolside, in a hotel, or on a cruise ship.

❧773❧

Q If the marriage ceremony will be held in a relatively open space, how should the setting be arranged?

A If there is no physical structure, a focal point for the service must be created. A gazebo can be constructed, as well as a platform with columns to hold candles.

❧774❧

Q What is the purpose of aisle ribbons?

A As part of the decorations of the ceremony site, the bride may opt to designate the front pews reserved for the wedding party and members of the immediate family with decorative ribbons.

∽775∼

*Q*What provisions should be made to accommodate guests at a unique ceremony site?

*A*Seating for all guests is a basic requirement, along with sturdy footing for the guests to take their places, rest room facilities, and parking.

∽776∾

Q What provisions should be made regarding parking?

A There should be enough reserved parking spaces in front of the church or synagogue for all the cars necessary to transport members of the wedding party. Special parking permits may be required.

∽777∾

Q What provisions should be made for a candlelight wedding?

A Fire officials should be consulted to determine the proper number and placement of candles.

∽778∾

Q What provisions should be made for an outdoor wedding?

A A tent or alternative site should be prepared in the event that inclement weather sets in.

∽779∾

Q In what ways can the bride honor her mother and
future mother-in-law at the wedding?

A Many brides will honor their mother by carrying a
special item like a handkerchief or family Bible as
they are wed. Other brides will present a flower
from their bouquet to their own mother during the
processional and one to their new mother-in-law
before the recessional.

∽780∾

Q In what ways can the bride and groom honor
deceased parents or grandparents in their marriage ceremony?

A A special notation of reverence for deceased family members can be discreetly included in the
wedding program or can be expressed in a special
prayer offered by the officiant.

∽781∾

Q What is the order of the recessional?

The recessional is led by the newlyweds, who are followed by the child attendants, the honor attendants, and pairs of bridesmaids and groomsmen.

782

Q How are guests dismissed from the marriage ceremony?

A After the wedding party has departed from the sanctuary, two ushers return to the front of the church or synagogue to lead the dismissal of guests. The bride's parents are the first to leave, followed by the groom's parents, and a filing out of the guests from the front row to the back.

783

Q What instructions should be given to the photographer covering the marriage ceremony?

A The wedding coordinator at the church or synagogue or the officiant can advise the bridal couple regarding rules governing picture taking in the house of worship. Some officiants do not allow picture taking during the ceremony, while others may simply forbid the use of flash photography.

∽784∾

Q What instructions should be given to the florist?

A The wedding coordinator at the church or synagogue can provide guidance about the size and
the number of the floral arrangements used to
decorate the ceremony site. Many churches and
synagogues have restrictions on the size and
placement of floral displays. In addition, the coordinator can confirm where and when the flowers
for the ceremony should be delivered by the
florist.

∽785∾

Q What provisions should be made to handle children at the ceremony?

A Most couples will prefer that young children do
not disturb the solemnness of the ceremony and
will arrange for a child-care area at a nearby location, manned by experienced baby-sitters.

∽786∾

Q Should the guest register be placed at the ceremony site?

Among several choices for placing the guestbook, the vestibule of the church, synagogue, or other ceremony site may be an ideal location for guests to sign the register upon arrival. The guest register may also be presented at the reception site.

787

When should the wedding party be invited to sign the guest register?

With all the excitement of the big day, the wedding party should be invited to sign the guestbook at the wedding rehearsal.

788

Is it acceptable for the guests to be welcomed at a reception before the marriage ceremony?

If most of the guests are not acquainted, especially if the wedding brings together two distant families, it might be a good idea to have a preceremony reception. This simple gathering is intended to offer the opportunity for the guests to meet each other, and can be complete with champagne, punch or coffee, and tea.

⊙789⊙

Q Is it acceptable for the guests to throw rice or bird-seed after the marriage ceremony?

A Most churches, synagogues, or alternative sites have designated rules governing what can be thrown at the bride and groom while they are leaving the reception for their honeymoon. It is best to check with the clergy or officiant on what the choices may be. Some alternatives to throwing rice or birdseed are flower petals, potpourri, or blowing soap bubbles. However, soap bubbles can stain some dress fabrics, so the bride should check with the bridal consultant to make sure the bridal gown will not be ruined by soap stains.

❧790❧

Q What provisions should be made if rice or bird-seed will be thrown after the ceremony?

A Many locations will insist that a custodial service clean up the remaining residue after the toss of rice or birdseed.

❧791❧

Q How should people dress for the rehearsal and rehearsal dinner?

A The attire should reflect the setting of the rehearsal and the dinner. The bride-and groom-to-be need to inform all participants of the appropriate dress and location of both the rehearsal and dinner.

❧792❧

Q Who should participate in the wedding rehearsal?

A In addition to the wedding party and the clergyperson, all musicians and soloists should be present to perform. The wedding coordinator of the church or synagogue should preside over the rehearsal.

∽793∾

Q How much time should be allowed for the rehearsal?

A The average rehearsal will require at least an hour of time to run through the entire ceremony and allow the wedding party to practice the processional and recessional several times.

∽794∾

Q If the church or synagogue has two aisles, how are the processional and recessional staged?

A With two aisles, the processional ascends the left aisle and the recessional descends the right aisle.

∽795∾

Q Can the receiving line be staged at the ceremony site following the wedding service?

A Although holding the receiving line at the ceremony site often delays the beginning of the reception, it may be more convenient for all the parents to join the bride and groom to greet guests immediately after the service.

∞796∞

Q What preparations should be made for a double wedding?

A A major consideration in planning a double wedding is to secure a ceremony site that is large enough to accommodate both wedding parties and all the guests.

∞797∞

Q What is the order of the processional at a double wedding?

A The two grooms take their place on either side of the clergyperson with their respective best man at their side. If the brides are sisters, the oldest usually enters first and takes her place on the left side, preceded by her bridesmaids and honor attendant. The younger sister's attendants enter, and she follows, taking her place on the right side. Each couple completes each portion of the ceremony in turn.

∞798∞

Q What is the order of the recessional at a double wedding?

A After the final blessing is bestowed over both couples, the older sister and her new husband exit first, followed by the younger sister and her new husband. Alternating between the two wedding parties, the honor attendants recess, followed by pairs of the bridesmaids and groomsmen.

∞799∞

Q What is the order of the recessional at a military wedding?

A The groom's fellow officers who serve as ushers recess and create their formation either at the back of the church or on the front steps of the church. The head usher commands the unit to draw their swords and each usher raises his saber in his right hand with the cutting edge facing up. As the bride and groom pass through the arch, it is customary for the last swordsman to affectionately tap the bride on her shoulder with his saber. The honor attendants and pairs of bridesmaids and groomsmen also pass through the arch.

∞800∞

Q What is the tradition of the bride being given away?

Reminiscent of the days when a bride was sold by her father to the prospective groom, the rite today is a sign of the father entrusting his beloved daughter to the care of her husband-to-be.

∽801∾

Q What is the tradition of the kiss at the conclusion of the wedding service?

A The kiss symbolizes the first time that these bodies are united as husband and wife, and represents the seal of the bargain.

∽802∾

Q What is the tradition behind the ringing of church bells at the conclusion of the marriage ceremony?

A Following the solemn wedding service, the church bells are rung as a joyous way to frighten away demons who might threaten the newlyweds.

12

The Wedding Reception

∞803∞

Q What factors should a couple consider when choosing the location for their reception?

A After developing a list of potential locations within close proximity of the ceremony site, a couple should seek out a reception facility that mirrors the formality of the wedding celebration and has the capacity to accommodate the estimated guest list.

∞804∞

Q What portion of the wedding budget should be devoted to the reception?

A The cost of the wedding reception typically represents the largest portion of the wedding expenses, commanding between one-third and one-half of the wedding budget.

∞805∞

Q What guideline should be followed regarding the distance between the locations for the marriage ceremony and the reception that follows?

As a general recommendation, the travel time between the ceremony and reception sites should be no more than a half hour drive.

 How does the atmosphere of the reception site contribute to the overall enjoyment of the wedding celebration?

 The guests will no doubt appreciate beautiful surroundings that continue the theme imbued at the ceremony and are staffed by professionals who have anticipated all of the facets of superior guest service.

12

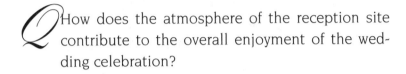

 In addition to a hotel or catering hall, what types of locations may be suitable for the reception site?

 Private clubs, hotels, restaurants, and the church social hall are the most common choices for the reception site. Among the most popular alternative reception sites are a museum or historic landmark, a garden or the out-of-doors, or a boat or yacht.

∞808∞

Q What factors should be considered when visiting a potential reception site?

A After determining that the location reflects the desired theme for the wedding and has adequate space to comfortably accommodate all the guests, the couple should research the cost of using the facilities for the desired amount of time, the options for food service, the staff available to service the guests, the opportunity to personalize the event, and any regulations that govern use of the site.

The couple should inquire about the availability of a wedding package.

∞809∞

Q What steps should be taken in booking the reception site?

A Most public facilities will provide a standard contract of service to be signed and will require a deposit to secure the desired date.

∞810∞

Q What types of food service should a couple consider for the reception?

A The time of day coupled with the degree of formality of the celebration will indicate the appropriate food presentation. The most formal affair usually offers a seated meal, while less formal options include a cocktail buffet, luncheon, brunch, or tea.

∞811∞

Q What are the characteristics of a very formal reception?

A A very formal reception occurs at noon or in the evening, complete with exquisite floral decorations; a cocktail reception; an elegantly set, multi-course meal with place cards and menu cards; and live entertainment for dancing.

∞812∞

Q What are the characteristics of a semiformal reception?

A A semiformal reception features a seated meal or a buffet, assigned tables for guests with floral centerpieces or the like, and live music.

❧813❧

Q What are the characteristics of an informal reception?

A Informal receptions are the perfect conclusion to an intimate wedding with a small guest list. The food service is typically light, including cocktails and finger foods, a simple buffet, or simply wedding cake, and champagne. The setting is casual with uncomplicated decorations.

❧814❧

Q What are the two major types of caterers?

A On-site caterers operate as a service arm of a facility, such as a hotel or private club. Off-premise caterers are independent food specialists who can create the menu as well as prepare and serve the meal.

❧815❧

Q How much flexibility can an on-site caterer provide?

A Most on-site caterers preside over sophisticated operations that thrive from the challenge of a unique wedding celebration. Nevertheless, an independent caterer may have more immediate access to a wider range of options.

∽816∽

Q What topics should be covered in the initial meeting with a potential caterer?

A At the introductory meeting with the caterer the bride should describe her image of the food to be served at the reception and provide all of the details that have already been determined. In addition to menu items, other topics for conversation include the methods of food presentation, the number of expected guests, seating plans, and the budget.

∽817∽

Q How does a couple determine the menu to be served at the wedding?

A Virtually all professional caterers will be able to provide a variety of suggested menus that have been enjoyed at previous wedding receptions. Most couples will want to personalize their meal service with some of their favorite foods or some ethnic dishes that reflect their family heritage.

❧818❧

Q How does a couple determine whether to offer a sit-down meal or buffet at the reception?

A Sit-down meals lend a more formal tone to the reception, while a buffet works well for more informal weddings where the guests can mingle throughout the party. The makeup of the guest list may influence a couple to provide a waiter-served meal with assigned seats for the comfort of the mature guests.

❧819❧

Q How can buffet service be designed to satisfy a larger guest list?

A The secret to a successful buffet is to assure an ample number of stations for guests to quickly serve themselves. It's a good idea for the caterer to set up duplicate stations on opposite sides of the banquet room.

❧820❧

Q How many waiters are necessary at the reception?

Most professional caterers assign one waiter for each ten to fifteen guests. While two-thirds of the wait staff is devoted to presenting food to the guests, the other waiters are passing beverages, replenishing food, or clearing dishes.

∞821∞

What kind of follow-up meetings take place once the caterer has been selected?

A complete menu and contract of all the details related to the food service should give way for a second meeting with the caterer that also typically features a tasting of the planned meal.

Another meeting will most likely be held about two weeks before the wedding to confirm the final head count and any last-minute changes.

∞822∞

What is the purpose of a tasting?

A tasting is typically hosted by the caterer for the bride, groom, and her parents as a dress rehearsal for service of the wedding meal. The meal begins with a sampling of assorted appetizers under consideration for the hors d'oeuvres presented before the meal. A salad course may be offered with several different dressings, and the top entrée choices are presented with different sauces and a variety of potato and vegetable dishes. The tasting concludes with a dessert sampler.

⁊823ᷜ

Q At what point in the wedding planning does the caterer require a deposit?

A In order to secure the best caterer, a bride may be required to place a nominal deposit that reserves the services of the caterer and his or her staff on the specific date as soon as she learns of the caterer's availability on her planned wedding day. A 50 percent deposit of the projected catering bill is typically placed with the final head count about a week or two before the wedding, with the balance due at or just before the reception.

⁊824ᷜ

Q What elements are included on the caterer's bill?

A In addition to the food and service charges on the caterer's bill are gratuities and taxes. Most businesses add gratuities of 15 percent of the food and service charges.

⟜825⟞

Q What unusual fees might occur from the caterer?

A A bride should anticipate overtime rates and damage allowances.

⟜826⟞

Q What refreshments should be served during the cocktail hour?

A The traditional fare at cocktail receptions include passed hors d'oeuvres that are bite-sized and easy to handle and champagne with an optional full bar. Nonalcoholic beverages, juices, and sodas should also be available.

⟜827⟞

Q Under what circumstances may the reception include a cash bar?

A A cash bar is considered in poor taste under any circumstance.

828

Q How many hors d'oeuvres should be prepared for the cocktail hour?

A With the anticipation of a multicourse dinner, each guest typically consumes an average of two to four servings of passed hors d'oeuvres along with a sampling from any individual chef's station.

829

Q Is it necessary to provide guests with a choice of entrée at the reception?

A Most caterers will design a menu that appeals to the majority of tastes. Since it may be awkward for the servers to offer a choice of meat, poultry, or fish entrées, the menu might include one food for the main course and another for the appetizer. A more formal reception meal might include a medallion of meat, poultry, and fish on each plate.

830

Q What foods are appropriate for a reception buffet?

The menu for a wedding buffet is similar to the traditional seated meal, including appetizers, salads, entrées, and desserts.

∽831∾

What foods are appropriate for a reception brunch?

A wedding brunch may be served at receptions scheduled for the late morning or early afternoon, including traditional egg dishes, fresh fruits, and breakfast breads.

∽832∾

What foods are appropriate for a reception tea?

A selection of finger sandwiches and scones are the traditional bounty served at afternoon teatime, along with fancy cookies or petits fours.

∽833∾

How can the food presentation at a wedding reception reflect the season of the celebration?

A Brides marrying during the springtime will enjoy seeing the foods in their wedding meal garnished with fresh edible flowers, while summertime wedding meals may begin with a chilled fruit soup. Miniature pumpkins filled with rice or vegetables offer a colorful decoration to the autumn reception plate, while warm fruit desserts are especially delicious at a winter wedding.

∞834∞

Q Is it the caterer's responsibility to provide the wedding cake?

A Although some large catering businesses employ a pastry chef on the staff, many caterers prefer to work with an independent cake baker. If the bride has a preference for a particular pastry chef, she should discuss her ideas with her caterer during the initial meeting.

∞835∞

Q How should the wedding cake be displayed at the reception?

A A special cake table is traditionally placed near the front of the reception site, decorated in a similar theme as the guest tables.

∽836∾

Q When should the wedding cake be served at the reception?

A The wedding cake should be cut as guests are finishing their meal.

∽837∾

Q What are the traditions related to the cutting of the cake?

A The groom traditionally places his hand over the bride's as a symbol of his desire to take care of her. It is also said that the bride's hand must be the first to cut the cake.

∽838∾

Q How should the newlyweds serve the first piece of cake to each other?

A The bride and groom hold the cake knife together, with the groom's hand placed over the bride's, as they make a slice in a bottom layer of the wedding cake. A dessert plate holds this first slice of cake and each offers a small bite to the other.

839

Q What is the tradition behind the bride and groom sharing the first taste of wedding cake by feeding each other?

A The ancient Greeks and Romans believed that the joint partaking of the cake created a magic bonding. The sweetness symbolized the couple's future happiness and the grain held the promise of a fruitful union.

840

Q Are the bride and groom responsible for cutting the wedding cake for guests?

A Usually, a close friend or member of the wait staff will continue cutting the cake for guests.

841

Q Is it acceptable to offer dessert in addition to wedding cake at the reception?

A A popular trend at receptions is to present a light dessert that completes the meal, with wedding cake served later during the reception or boxed for guests to take home.

∞842∞

Q How should the groom's cake be presented at the reception?

A Many couples will opt to offer their guests a choice of tasting the bride's cake, groom's cake, or a combination of the two. The groom's cake should be placed on a similar table next to the bride's cake.

∞843∞

Q What special food provisions should be made for the newlyweds?

A Since many newlyweds find themselves too excited to enjoy the reception meal, many caterers will arrange a picnic basket for the couple to take away as they leave for the honeymoon.

∞844∞

Q How should the head table be arranged?

A The newlyweds and their attendants may be seated at round tables placed in the front of the reception site, or they may be seated at a long table that faces the wedding guests.

The bride is usually flanked by the best man and the maid or matron of honor sits next to the groom.

⊗845⊗

Q How many guests should be seated at each table at the reception?

A Large round tables can usually accommodate eight to ten guests.

⊗846⊗

Q What style of floral arrangements are best suited to reception tables?

A Table centerpieces should not obstruct eye contact among the guests at the table, and are either low or placed on pedestals above eye level.

⊗847⊗

Q What considerations should be made in choosing the flowers for the table centerpieces?

A Scent is an important consideration since the guests should enjoy a fragrant floral display while not being overpowered by the aroma.

∞848∞

Q How can floral touches be used in presenting the food at the reception?

A The florist should work closely with the caterer to design floral arrangements or topiaries for the buffet stations, and may be able to provide simple adornments for the trays of hors d'oeuvres or edible flowers for the guest plates. The florist may also design floral touches that accent the wedding cake table.

∞849∞

Q When is it appropriate to use place cards, and how are they presented to guests?

A Place cards are used whenever a substantial meal is provided at the reception and seats are planned for the guests. A draped table complete with oversized centerpiece should be erected outside the reception area to hold the alphabetically arranged place cards. At a formal reception, the place card should correspond with name cards at each place setting at the assigned table. At a semiformal reception, the place card simply identifies the assigned table.

∞850∞

Q When is it appropriate to use menu cards, and how are they presented to guests?

A Menu cards are only appropriate at very formal weddings and should be styled similar to the place card. Menu cards may be placed on the charger of each place setting, may be positioned between two place settings, or may be stood back-to-back in the center of the table.

∞851∞

Q How can the reception tables be personalized for the reception?

A The guests' tables are usually draped in a full-length tablecloth with a decorative overlay. The table linens should complement the color scheme of the setting as well as coordinate with the color theme of the wedding. Many reception sites offer a selection of fabrics for slipcovered chairs or chair cushions.

Napkins at each place setting can be wrapped with ribbon or lace for a romantic touch, or crisply folded for a more tailored appeal. In addition, favors at each place setting provide a special touch.

∽852∾

Q What factors influence the design of the center-piece of a reception table?

A The centerpiece always blends with the formality and the colors of the wedding, and is sized to not obstruct conversation among the guests. The materials in the centerpiece should offer a pleas-ing, understated aroma.

∽853∾

Q What are some suggested favors for each place setting?

A Placement of the place card or menu card in a frame is an elegant favor, as are tiny bud vases with a single bloom. Candies or sugared almonds presented in tiny boxes or gathered in circles of tulle tied with ribbon are the most popular favors.

∽854∾

Q What is the tradition behind the popular tulle-wrapped bundle of sugared almonds?

A Italian custom says this confection represents the sweetness and the bitterness of married life.

∽855∾

Q When is candlelight appropriate for the reception tables?

A Receptions commencing after five o'clock are often enhanced with the use of candlelight. The florist may incorporate tapered candles in the floral centerpiece or may surround the centerpiece with tiny votives.

∽856∾

Q How important is a coat check facility?

A A coat check facility should be planned for every reception, in anticipation of housing coats and outerwear for cold weather as well as umbrellas on a rainy day.

∽857∾

Q Is it necessary to have a receiving line?

A While some brides prefer not to stage a formal scene, the structured receiving line is really the best way to ensure that the newlyweds greet each guest and make them feel welcome. This also enables out-of-town guests and infrequently seen relatives a chance to meet individual members of the wedding party who have not yet been introduced.

∽858∾

Q When should the receiving line be scheduled?

A The optimal time for the receiving line is at the beginning of the reception. Following the marriage ceremony, guests can make their way to the reception site and enjoy a beverage and selection of hors d'oeuvres while the wedding party shoots the group pictures. Once the newlyweds arrive at the reception, they may gather with their parents to greet guests in the transition to the meal service.

859

Q Can the receiving line be staged at the church or synagogue immediately following the marriage ceremony?

A In a limited number of situations this may work, but in most instances the receiving line setup after the ceremony results in a slowed departure of guests from the church or synagogue and delay in beginning the reception.

860

Q What is the proper order of participants in the receiving line?

A The bride's mother, who serves as the hostess of the reception, leads the line, followed by the groom's father and mother, the bride's father, the bride and groom, the maid or matron of honor, and the bridesmaids.

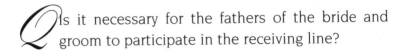

861

Q Is it necessary for the fathers of the bride and groom to participate in the receiving line?

A Some fathers of the bridal couple prefer not to be part of the receiving line, which can be simply managed with the two mothers at the head of the line. The bride's father, as host of the reception, should circulate among the guests and make sure that everything is running smoothly.

862

Q Is it necessary for the bride's attendants to participate in the receiving line?

A If the bride's attendants are her sisters and cousins who know many of the guests at the wedding, they should be part of the receiving line. If the bridal attendants are primarily friends from college who will not know many of the guests, it is not necessary for them to join the receiving line.

863

Q What should the bride do before the wedding to prepare for the receiving line?

It's a good idea to review the guest list with both mothers so that the guests' names and their proper pronunciations are fresh on everyone's minds.

Q Should the bride remove her gloves for the receiving line?

A Many brides appreciate wearing their gloves during the receiving line since they help to absorb hand perspiration. At the same time, the bride appears as elegant and graceful as the moment she entered the ceremony site.

❦865❧

Q How should the guest register be handled in conjunction with the receiving line?

A By placing the guest register at either the beginning or end of the receiving line, all the guests will have a chance to inscribe a personal message for the newlyweds.

❦866❧

Q What provisions should be made for the bride and groom while they participate in the receiving line?

A It is acceptable to have a glass of champagne or punch waiting on a nearby table, but it's advisable not to be drinking too often since it will slow the flow of the line.

❦867❧

Q What is the historical meaning of the wedding toast?

A The custom of proposing toasts originated in ancient France where a piece of toast was placed at the bottom of a wineglass to soak up the sediment. The competent toaster imbibed everything in his or her zeal to drain the glass.

868

Q Who typically offers a toast?

A The first toast to the bride and groom is made by the best man, followed by best wishes from close friends or relatives. The groom should then toast his bride, their parents, plus their friends and family members.

869

Q Can the bride offer a toast?

A The bride often offers a toast to her new husband, following the groom's toasts. However, it is not required that she offer a toast.

870

Q Who follows the bride's toast?

A The bride's father should follow the bride, continued by the groom's father, and other guests attending the wedding.

❧871❧

Q What advice should be given to those who want to offer a toast?

A Toasts should be short commentaries of less than five minutes, should never embarrass anyone, and should be prepared in advance.

❧872❧

Q When should the wedding toasts be scheduled?

A At a reception with a seated meal, the toasts may begin after all guests have taken their places and the first course has been presented.

❧873❧

Q At what point during the reception do the bride and groom share their first dance?

A The first dance usually follows the toasts, and may occur just before or immediately after the main course is served.

∞874∞

Q Is it acceptable for guests to begin dancing as soon as they arrive at the reception?

A The guests may enjoy dancing after they go through the receiving line while they wait for the bride and groom to greet all of the guests.

ೲ875ೲ

Q What is the order for the wedding party to dance following the bride and groom's first dance?

A The bride's father cuts in on the groom to dance with his daughter while the groom invites the bride's mother to be his guest on the dance floor. The groom's father then cuts in on the bride's father while the groom asks his mother to dance.

Following dances with their parents, the bride dances with the best man while the groom dances with the maid of honor. The entire wedding party joins the honor attendants for a short time before all the guests are invited to dance.

At some point during the reception, the bride should dance with each groomsman and the groom should dance with each bridesmaid.

ೲ876ೲ

Q What is the significance of the garter toss?

A In the days that men and women wore garters to hold up their stockings, the bride was often teased by the groomsmen who attempted to lift her skirt and steal her garters. Today the garter is often the "something blue" worn by the bride and is tossed by the groom.

⚮877⚮

Q What is the significance of the bouquet toss?

A In the eighteenth century as weddings took on a civilized tone, brides abdicated the practice of tossing their garters and substituted the custom with a toss of their bouquet.

⚮878⚮

Q What purpose does the bouquet toss serve today?

A A gracious way to signal the nearing of the end of the reception is with the tossing of the bride's bouquet.

⚮879⚮

Q When is the bride's garter thrown?

A This is usually done prior to the bouquet toss. The groom makes a big display of removing the bride's garter. The single male guests are gathered around the groom in preparation of receiving the toss. The lucky one to catch the garter is believed to be the next to marry.

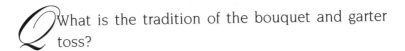

Q What is the tradition of the bouquet and garter toss?

A The lucky winner of the bouquet toss among the single, female guests at the reception and the lucky winner of the garter toss among the single, male guests are said to be the next to marry.

881

Q Is it necessary to toss the bouquet and garter at the reception?

A Some brides, particularly mature women who have planned a sophisticated wedding, prefer to skip this tradition.

882

Q Is it acceptable to set up a gift table at the reception?

A Traditional etiquette recommends that guests deliver their gifts to the bride in advance of the wedding day. Nevertheless, in today's busy lifestyle, some guests will bring their wedding gift to the reception, and brides may ask their caterer to provide a draped table that can be discreetly placed to hold those gifts.

∞883∞

Q Is it proper for the bride and groom to open gifts delivered to the reception?

A It is considered in poor taste for the newlyweds to open gifts with the guests. Gifts delivered to the reception should be transported to the bride's parents' home or to the newlyweds' home to be opened upon their return from the honeymoon.

∞884∞

Q What provisions should be made for a wedding reception held in a private home?

A Many brides enjoy the opportunity to celebrate their marriage at home, often with the help of a rented tent to accommodate ample space for guests. The florist can romanticize the setting with potted trees bathed in twinkling lights and fresh flowers. A rented dance floor should be placed near the front of the tent.

∞885∞

Q In what instances is it appropriate to issue separate invitations to the reception?

A For brides with divorced parents, it is not unusual for the bride's mother to issue invitations to the marriage ceremony and the bride's father to issue invitations to the reception.

If the marriage ceremony site can only accommodate immediate family members and close friends, it is acceptable to invite other relatives and friends to join in the reception.

∞886∞

Q What are the customs related to the conclusion of the reception?

A The tradition of showering the newlyweds with rice as they depart for the honeymoon anticipates the fruitfulness of the union. Today, birdseed, confetti, or dried flowers have replaced the rice.

The custom of tying shoes onto the back of the honeymoon getaway car dates back to when the father of the bride gave her shoes to her new husband, signifying that she was now the groom's property.

13

Cakes

∞887∞

Q What is the historical custom of serving cake at a wedding?

A The wedding cake originated in ancient cultures as a fertility rite for the newlyweds. From the offering of grain to the gods evolved the baking of cakes which were crumbled and broken over a bride's head to bless her with successful child-bearing. The ancient Romans dictated that when a bride was given to the groom by her father, the couple shared a ceremonial barley cake which was dedicated to the god Jupiter.

∞888∞

Q What is the most traditional wedding cake today?

A Unlike years ago when a vanilla cake frosted with white icing was the norm, today's brides are choosing wedding cakes created with style and imagination. Today's wedding cakes can be virtually any flavor (even deep chocolate) and accented by a sweet filling ranging from white chocolate mousse to raspberry.

Q Is it traditional for the bride's cake to be an all-white confection? **13**

A While bridal cakes in years past were typically created of white cake and icing, the modern-day wedding cake can be decorated in a full range of color to coordinate with the theme of the wedding celebration.

❧890❧

Q What is the first step brides should take in planning for their wedding cake?

A Brides should begin their cake planning with a
careful look at their wedding budget. Wedding
cakes can be expensive, priced at the upper end
from seven dollars to nine dollars per slice.

❧891❧

Q What factors influence the price of the wedding
cake?

A The size and cost of the wedding cake is first
determined by the number of guests. The most
basic flavors will cost less than creative combinations of flavors.

❧892❧

Q If any guests have dietary restrictions, should perhaps a sugar-free cake be provided?

A Many bakeries do make a sugar-free cake. The cost
may be more, but a smaller sized cake is all that is
necessary.

❦ 893 ❦

Q How does a bride decide which baker to choose?

A References are essential to determining the most competent baker. Most bakers can provide an album containing pictures of previous wedding cakes they've created.

❦ 894 ❦

Q What questions should the bride ask during her interview of a cake baker?

A The bride should ask about the ingredients that the baker prefers to use, looking for quality and freshness. If the wedding will take place during the summertime, the bride should ask if the baker will deliver the cake in a refrigerated truck.

❦ 895 ❦

Q Is it advisable to participate in a cake tasting?

A Similar to the tasting conducted when determining the reception menu, the bride, groom, and her parents should sample a variety of cake choices before placing the wedding cake order. Many professional cake bakers will host special tasting parties for engaged couples to be introduced to the wide assortment of cake, frosting, and filling flavors.

Q What information should the bride provide the cake baker?

A Besides the date, time, and location of the reception, the bride should tell the baker about as many details of the wedding as possible so that the cake created for the occasion is compatible with the theme of the day. Important facts include the number of invited guests, the colors of the wedding fashions, and the decorating theme of the reception site.

897

Q What services should the bride expect from her cake baker?

A Many bakers include delivery of the wedding cake as part of their service. The bride-to-be should ask whether the provision of a cake knife is part of the package.

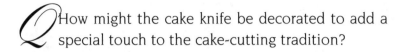

898

Q How might the cake knife be decorated to add a special touch to the cake-cutting tradition?

A A fresh flower tied to the knife handle is a charming accent as well as a delicate bow of ribbon.

899

Q What unexpected fees might be associated with the wedding cake?

A If the wedding cake is provided by a custom baker, the catering staff might assess a slicing fee to serve the cake.

900

Q When should the bride place the order for her wedding cake?

A Most bakers will require at least two months' notice to prepare the cake of her dreams. Since the best cake bakers are booked first, the bride should reserve the cake baker as soon as the wedding date is confirmed.

∞901∞

Q When is a deposit necessary to secure the services of the cake baker?

A A partial payment is a standard accompaniment to placing the order for the wedding cake. The balance is typically due on or just a few days before the wedding day.

∞902∞

Q Where should the wedding cake be placed at the reception site?

The wedding cake should be placed in a prominent, central location that can be easily viewed by the seated guests.

Q How should the wedding cake be presented at the reception?

 Most florists will assist the caterer to create a special cake table that coordinates with the other decorations at the reception site. In addition to the floral accents provided by the florist to decorate the cake table, many brides and maids encircle the top of the cake table with their bouquets. This practice produces a flower-filled setting for the wedding cake as well as allows the guests to admire the pretty bouquets.

Q What are some of the most popular combinations of cake and icing?

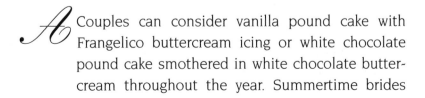 Couples can consider vanilla pound cake with Frangelico buttercream icing or white chocolate pound cake smothered in white chocolate buttercream throughout the year. Summertime brides

might enjoy a large strawberry shortcake lavished with fresh whipped cream and laden with sweet, ripe berries. Carrot cake with a smooth, cream cheese frosting or spice cake embedded with raisins and nuts and iced with a creamy amaretto frosting are perfect choices for an autumn wedding.

Q What is "ganache"?

A A popular cake covering or filling, ganache is made from melted chocolate, heavy cream, and flavoring.

Q What is "fondant"?

A Fondant is a rich, rolled frosting consisting of sugar, water, and other flavorings that provides a smooth, finished surface.

Q What are the most popular flavors of fillings for wedding cakes?

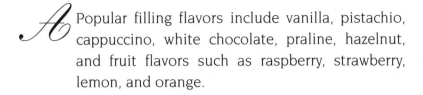 Popular filling flavors include vanilla, pistachio, cappuccino, white chocolate, praline, hazelnut, and fruit flavors such as raspberry, strawberry, lemon, and orange.

 Is it acceptable to choose a different flavor of cake for each layer of the wedding cake?

If the bride and groom have a hard time determining their favorite flavor of cake, filling, and frosting, they may choose to combine several compatible flavors in separate layers and allow the guests to select the type of cake they prefer.

Is there a proper shape for a wedding cake?

A wedding cake can be of any shape, including round, square, oblong, or heart-shaped.

What are the choices for decorating the cake?

Fresh flowers are the most popular accent to adorn wedding cakes, along with a favorite family heirloom cake top. The bride and groom may choose to start their own family tradition by choosing a new china or crystal ornament to top the cake.

Other popular looks include a cascade of sugar flowers, a fondant bow, or a bevy of polka dots.

Q What is a groom's cake?

A groom's cake is a popular Southern wedding custom, rooted from traditional European wedding celebrations, that is quickly gaining in popularity around the country. It is a special cake, usually chocolate and designed with the groom's personality in mind–his vocation, fraternity letters, or favorite recreational sport.

∞912∞

What other flavors besides chocolate are popular for the groom's cake?

Spice cake, carrot cake, and almond pound cake are some of the most popular choices for groom's cakes, although any favorite flavor of the groom should be considered.

∞913∞

When is it appropriate to present the groom's cake?

The groom's cake can be served for dessert at the rehearsal dinner or presented alongside the bride's wedding cake at the reception. If the couple choose to serve the bride's cake after the reception meal, the groom's cake may be placed in small gift boxes and distributed for guests to take home from the reception.

❦914❦

Q What is the tradition of the groom's cake?

A Legend suggests that the single woman who places a wrapped slice of the groom's cake beneath her pillow at bedtime will dream of her future husband.

❦915❦

Q What is the tradition of bridesmaids' charms in the wedding cake?

A The bride should ask her pastry chef to enclose a selection of silver charms attached to ribbon streamers in the frosting between the layers of the cake. Before the newlyweds share the first taste of the wedding cake, the maids are invited to choose a ribbon and pull out one of the charms. The charms are said to represent the promise of the future, including hope, love, good luck, next to marry, or old maid.

❦916❦

Q What is the protocol for serving the bride's cake at the reception?

The bride and groom should cut the first slice of the cake together, with his hand placed over hers on the cake knife.

∞917∞

Q Who should take the first taste of the wedding cake?

 The bride always samples the cake first before offering her groom a taste, a gesture derived from the ancient fertility rite.

∞918∞

Q Why do couples traditionally save the top layer of their wedding cake?

 The tradition of eating the top layer of wedding cake on the first anniversary of marriage is a recent bridal custom. It is said that a cake that withstands a year of storage and still tastes great will be the sign of a lasting marriage.

∞919∞

Q How should the top layer be handled after the wedding?

A After the reception, the top layer is carefully wrapped and placed in the couple's freezer. A few days before the first anniversary, the cake should be removed from the freezer and placed fully wrapped in the refrigerator to thaw.

❧920❧

Q If a family member or close friend celebrates a birthday on the wedding day, is it acceptable for the bride and groom to offer a special birthday cake for the occasion?

A It is indeed thoughtful to honor this special occasion with a candle-laden confection. Perhaps the caterer could present the birthday cake immediately after the bride and groom have shared their first slice of wedding cake while all the guests are gathered together.

14

The
Honeymoon

∞921∞

Q Who is responsible for paying for the honeymoon?

A Traditionally, the groom and his family are responsible for the cost of the honeymoon, although a growing number of newlyweds are assuming this expense. It is not unusual for the groom's family to provide the honeymoon as their gift to the bride and groom.

∞922∞

Q How do a bride and groom decide where to take their honeymoon?

A After months of wedding planning and the excitement of their big day, most couples look forward to quiet time to relax together in a quaint locale. Including even the most modest sports enthusiasts, many couples additionally seek out destinations and resorts with a romantic setting and a variety of entertainment and activities. Warm weather, close proximity to the beach, and exotic surroundings are other factors that often influence the destination choice.

∽923∾

Q What is the first step couples should take in planning the honeymoon?

A Before deciding on the destination, it's a good idea to establish a honeymoon budget. Once the couple have an idea of how much they can spend, they can begin to research their options.

14

∞924∞

Q What determines the "perfect" honeymoon?

A An ideal honeymoon satisfies the needs and expectations of both the bride and groom. If the couple share many mutual interests, then beginning to plan should be easy. If the couple's interests are varied, they need to identify what points each holds important and attempt to plan a vacation that incorporates the maximum number of priorities.

∞925∞

Q What factors should be included in making up the honeymoon budget?

A Among the basic expenses will be the cost of transportation to the destination plus taxis or an automobile rental, accommodations, meals, entertainment, activities, and tips.

∞926∞

Q What sources should engaged couples consult in beginning to plan their honeymoon?

A The "Honeymoon Travel" section in each issue of **Elegant Bride** offers a wealth of information on a variety of destinations as well hints for making the most of this special time. Bookstores and the local library offer guidebooks on destinations, often complete with lists of special points of interest and accommodations. Tourist bureaus can provide significant information about international destinations.

927

Q What is the advantage of using a travel agent to make the arrangements for the honeymoon?

A First, the travel agent should be a source of information about your chosen location, with suggestions of places to see and things to do. Most likely the travel agency maintains an assortment of brochures, reference books, and videos for their clients.

Professional travel agents should be able to obtain special fares and details of honeymoon packages, as well as have a better chance of securing reservations at a highly sought-after hotel or resort.

If traveling by air, a travel agent should be able to make advance seat reservations and in some cases provide advance boarding passes.

Ꮽ928Ꮧ

Q What considerations should be made in choosing a travel agent?

A A good travel agent will listen to the travelers' plans and then ask questions to be sure that all details of this important vacation are addressed. Consult family members and friends for recommendations of their favorite travel professional.

Ꮽ929Ꮧ

Q Do travel agents charge a fee for their services?

A Engaged couples should inquire about potential fees resulting from the planning of their honeymoon. Traditionally, the services offered by travel agents are provided free of charge to the consumer. Agents typically earn commissions from the airlines, cruise lines, tour companies, hotels, and automobile rental agencies with whom they book reservations.

Ꮽ930Ꮧ

Q What features are included in a honeymoon package?

A Hotel and resort honeymoon packages may include special accommodations in a honeymoon suite, complimentary champagne and flowers, and a gift from the manager.

Some airline honeymoon packages combine air travel with accommodations and ground transportation.

∞931∞

Q What is an "all-inclusive" honeymoon package?

A An all-inclusive honeymoon typically refers to a prepaid package that includes transportation, accommodations, meals, sports and entertainment, gratuities, and taxes.

Couples should be sure to check any exceptions that may result in additional charges, such as telephone surcharges, room service, alcoholic beverages, laundry, and special health/fitness services.

∞932∞

Q How much should honeymooners tip restaurant personnel?

A Good service by a waiter or waitress deserves a tip of at least 15 percent to 20 percent of the bill before taxes. In many foreign countries, a service charge is automatically applied to the bill.

∞933∞

Q How much should honeymooners tip hotel personnel?

A The doorman should receive at least one dollar each time a taxi is hailed or the guests are assisted with either their arrival at or departure from the hotel. The bellman should receive a dollar for each piece of luggage delivered to the room upon arrival or to the lobby upon departure. The room attendant should receive one or two dollars per day. The valet attendant should receive a dollar each time the guests picks up their car.

∞934∞

Q How much should honeymooners tip transportation personnel?

A A taxi driver should receive at least 15 percent of the fare, excluding tolls.
    The tip for a limousine driver is typically included in the bill.

∽935∾

Q What are the various meal plans that may be available as part of a honeymoon package?

A The American Plan provides three meals per day. The Modified American Plan provides two meals per day, typically breakfast and dinner. The European Plan offers no meals. The Continental Plan provides a simple breakfast.

∽936∾

Q What types of meal service are offered by the major airlines?

A Travelers on major airlines may be able to request special meals at no additional charge, including vegetarian, kosher, seafood, and fruit, by placing their choices in advance.

∽937∾

Q How should the expenses related to the honeymoon be covered?

A A major credit card should be used to secure all travel and lodging reservations. It's usually advantageous to have the power of a credit card company in settling a dispute, if one arises, with an airline, hotel, or travel agent.

∽938∾

Q After the honeymoon is booked by the travel agent, can changes be made?

A When a reservation is booked in advance, a fee may be required to make changes to the original request. Occasionally, a reduced airfare may prove so much lower than the original fare that the travelers will still enjoy a savings after the change fee is applied.

∽939∾

Q Is it necessary for honeymooners to check in with the gate agent if their airline tickets include advance boarding passes?

A Yes, since late-arriving passengers may be withheld from overbooked flights.

∽940∾

Q What obligation does a major airline have to travelers scheduled on a canceled flight?

A The air carriers are legally required to provide alternative transportation for the most expedient arrival, including the possibility of transferring the passengers to another airline.

∞941∞

Q How much luggage is allowed per passenger on a major airline?

A The airlines generally limit each passenger to two checked bags weighing no more than seventy pounds and one carry-on bag. The travel agent can confirm the amount of luggage allowed.

∞942∞

Q What steps should be taken when a piece of luggage is lost by the airline?

A Passengers with lost luggage will be required to submit a description of their suitcases and the contents to the air carrier. Most airlines are liable up to a certain amount per bag, as noted on the traveler's airline ticket. Travelers carrying more than the airline's liability are advised to secure additional luggage insurance.

∞943∞

Q What items should travelers place in their carry-on bag?

A All tickets and travel documents, personal identification, valuables, and personal necessities should be packed in a carry-on bag, including passport and visas, medication and eyeglasses, money, jewelry, and a camera.

Many experienced travelers also include toiletries, additional clothing, and snacks.

∞944∞

Q What items should travelers to a foreign country include in their luggage?

A Although some hotels and resorts provide hair dryers in the bath, travelers may choose to carry an adapter for their personal appliances.

It's often a good idea to obtain a small amount of foreign currency for use upon arrival at the airport.

∽945∾

Q What fees are incurred in securing travel documents for an international destination?

A A standard fee is required to obtain a passport, and some visa applications require payment. When applying for a passport, allow at least six week for processing. In addition, some foreign countries impose a departure tax that is typically paid at the airport at the beginning of the return trip.

∽946∾

Q How can a couple learn about accommodations in the area they plan to honeymoon?

A Travel agents can provide a list of recommended lodging, and may be able to provide a personal endorsement from their own experience or the experience of previous honeymoon travelers.

Most destination guidebooks include descriptions and ratings of the lodging choices, while tourist bureaus can provide information on international accommodations.

❦947❦

Q What is the purpose of guaranteeing the first night's accommodations on a credit card?

A A guaranteed reservation assures availability of requested accommodations if the travelers arrive late, traditionally after 6:00 P.M.

❦948❦

Q What documents are required for traveling abroad?

A The tourist bureau of the destination country can provide a complete list of necessary documents. In addition to a passport, some locations also require a visa and certain inoculations.

❦949❦

Q Where should honeymooners file applications for obtaining a passport?

A Passport applications can be filed at regional passport offices as well as many federal and state courthouses and post offices.

⌒950⌒

Q What items must honeymooners provide in order to obtain a passport?

A To obtain a passport, honeymooners must provide proof of citizenship, most commonly available from a certified copy of their birth certificate, along with a completed application form, two passport photos, and fee payment.

⌒951⌒

Q What is a visa?

A Certain countries require travelers to carry a visa, or written permission, during their visit. Visas can be obtained by sending an application form with the travelers' passports to the consulate of the country to be visited. Travelers should allow six weeks to secure the necessary paperwork.

⌒952⌒

Q How much time is required to confirm travel on international airlines?

A All international flights require confirmation seventy-two hours before departure, even if the travelers are in possession of their tickets and boarding passes.

∞953∞

Q What factors contribute to the wide range of pricing for a honeymoon cruise?

A Cabin location and the quality of service provided are the basis of cruise line pricing. Other important variables are the ports of the itinerary and the dates of travel.

∞954∞

Q What costs are included in the price of a honey-moon cruise?

A Standard provisions include cabin accommodations, meals and snacks, sports facilities, and entertainment.

∞955∞

Q What costs are extra to the honeymoon cruise package?

A Added expenses may include land excursions, alcoholic beverages, room service, laundry, and special health/fitness services. Gratuities for the staff are offered to servers at the end of the cruise, typically placed in a small envelope and presented directly to the person.

∞956∞

Q What are the appropriate tips for cruise line personnel?

A The cabin steward and the dining room waiter should each receive four to six dollars per day.

Busboys should be given two to four dollars per day. Bartenders, wine stewards, and room service waiters should be tipped at the time of service.

∞957∞

Q What special requests might couples planning a honeymoon cruise make in advance of the departure?

A Many cabins are equipped with single beds, although other sizes may be available by request.

∞958∞

Q What arrangements must be made in order to be married at the same location as the honeymoon?

A Many resorts are appropriately staffed in order to assist couples interested in hosting their wedding in an exotic location. The couple should allow as much time as possible for the on-site wedding coordinator to orchestrate all the details, assuring adequate time to fulfill any legal requirements.

On-site wedding coordinators can secure the proper clergyperson or officiant as well as arrange for the flowers, food and beverages, and photography.

❦959❦

Q. What are the legal requirements for marrying outside the United States?

A. Legal requirements vary by country, although several general prerequisites apply to many locations. Typically, the engaged couple must complete a formal application, complete with birth certificates, and divorce papers. In some cases the document must be notarized, and a blood test may be required. The waiting period for the issuance of a marriage license may range from twenty-four hours to a few weeks.

❦960❦

Q. What is the derivation of "honeymoon"?

A. Some believe that the first month of marriage is the sweetest, while others believe the term evolved from the Anglo-Saxon tradition of a newly married couple retreating to a private locale and drinking mead, a fermented drink made from honey, for thirty days, or the passing of a moon, after the wedding.

Your First Home

961

Q What is the significance of carrying the bride over the threshold?

A One of the most celebrated wedding traditions dates back to the ancient Romans who believed in the precaution against evil demons lurking around the front doorway to trap the happy couple.

962

Q What are the basic elements of a healthy marriage?

A Besides love, the foundation for a strong relationship is built on patience, communication, and understanding.

963

Q How does a couple's relationship change as they move from being engaged to being married?

A For most newlyweds, the exchange of wedding rings cements the commitment they pledged to be responsible to each other. Each spouse is the primary source of comfort and support for his or her partner.

964

Q What role does communication play in a marriage?

A Good communication feeds a marriage through the exchange of words and emotions. Although both the bride and groom may find it necessary to learn to overlook annoying habits in their mates, it is not a good idea to refrain from confronting major issues and decisions together.

965

Q How can a couple judge the development of their relationship as married partners?

A The newlyweds' success as a couple will stem from each of their opportunities to grow individually as well as their ability to grow as a couple. They should allow each other personal time while also making plans to enjoy activities together.

15

Q How can couples minimize the frustration of learning how to live with each other every day after the honeymoon?

A In a lot of cases, newlyweds will admit to possessing opposite personalities and acknowledging that their spouse embodies traits that are repressed in their own lifestyle. In addition to assuring mutual tolerance, the partners should benefit from respect and grace under pressure.

Q How can couples keep the romance of their courtship and honeymoon alive in their marriage after the wedding?

A In recreating the activities that they enjoyed while dating, newlyweds can maintain the excitement of their relationship together. The secret lies in making plans to spend quality time together doing a mutually enjoyable activity. Many couples set aside time each week for a "date" of dinner and a movie, a weekend afternoon of bike riding or in-line skating, or a walk in the park with a picnic lunch.

Q What steps should be taken to maintain a balance between marriage and career?

A It's a good idea to regularly share thoughts on how both the bride's and groom's professional endeavors affect their daily lives and their long-term goals. Expectations before the wedding regarding the place of work in the marriage may need to be updated once the couple establish their daily routine.

Certainly the couple must strive to find time to spend together, either joining in an athletic activity or sharing quiet time.

Q How can couples increase their enjoyment of entertaining at home?

A Familiarity breeds comfort, and invitations to family members and friends are the perfect way to develop skills as a host and hostess. The delight in seeing guests enjoy themselves and the company of others may best be achieved by engaging in an occasion that is comfortable for everyone.

∽970∾

Q How should newlyweds extend invitations to a few couples for a casual dinner at home?

A Invitations to a casual occasion are typically telephoned, or may be written on informal notecards.

∽971∾

Q What steps should be taken to make sure the dinner party gets off on the right track?

A It may be helpful to the hostess to think about a theme for the party and plan the table decor and menu around the concept.

When the guests arrive they should be greeted by both the host and hostess. If one spouse is involved in finalizing preparation of the meal, he or she may return to the kitchen quickly after exchanging pleasantries.

When it's time for the meal to be served, the hostess invites guests to the dining area and directs where everyone should sit.

∽972∾

Q How can a couple maximize the pleasure of guests dining in their home?

A A pretty table setting seems to make the food both look and taste better. Table linens and table decorations should complement the occasion.

Background lighting and music should both be lowered as guests are seated to enhance the mood and facilitate lively conversation.

∞973∞

Q How can hollowware be put to imaginative use throughout the home?

A These serving objects–bowls, pitchers, trays, etc.–should be used as decorative accessories rather than relegated to the closet or cupboard. For example, a bowl can hold fruit, candy, pot-pourri, and more, while a pitcher can double as a vase for cut flowers.

∞974∞

Q What is the most inexpensive way to change the look of the newlyweds' registered table setting?

A In building a wardrobe for the tabletop, savvy brides depend upon a selection of different colors and styles of table linens to change the mood of their entertaining through color and design. A solid palette adds a classic tone, while pure linen adds a touch of formality. A combination of colors and patterns adds a festive, casual ambiance.

∽975∾

Q What is the rule of thumb related to centerpieces on a dining table?

A The first requirement is that the centerpiece fit the table and the occasion, providing a focal point to the table and reflecting the hosts' personal style and creativity. A fussy floral arrangement should be reserved for formal dining or for a buffet table. Candles burnt during a meal should have flames positioned above or below the guests' line of vision.

∽976∾

Q How can a table be set for the most ease by the guests?

A A table set with the minimum amount of tableware will be the most approachable and the least confusing for the guests.

ᘒ977ᘔ

Q How should the tableware be set for an informal luncheon?

A For a simple luncheon that includes a salad as the first course, set the place setting, from the left: folded napkin, salad fork, dinner fork, dinner plate, dinner knife, and teaspoon. The water goblet and wineglass are placed at the upper right of the place setting.

ᘒ978ᘔ

Q How should the tableware be set for a formal luncheon?

A For a formal luncheon with a salad as the first course, set the place setting, from the left: salad fork, dinner fork, dinner plate topped with the folded luncheon napkin, dinner knife, and salad knife. The water goblet and wineglass are placed at the upper right of the place setting.

ᘒ979ᘔ

Q How should the table be set for an informal dinner?

For a casual dinner that presents the salad course after the main course, set the place setting, from the left: salad plate, dinner fork, salad fork, dinner plate, salad knife, and dinner knife. The bread-and-butter plate with butter knife is placed at the upper left of the place setting, with the water goblet and wineglass at the upper right. The napkin should be arranged in a decorative fold and can be placed on or above the dinner plate, or may be placed in the goblet.

How should the table be set for an informal dessert?

The dessert course of an informal meal is typically presented after the preceding course has been cleared. The dessert fork and spoon are delivered to the table on the plate, and the diner places the flatware on the table. The coffee cup is delivered with the spoon resting on the saucer.

How should the table be set for a formal dinner?

For a formal, five-course dinner including soup, seafood dish, entrée, salad, and dessert, set the place setting, from the left: fish fork, dinner fork, salad fork, service plate topped with the folded dinner napkin, salad knife, dinner knife, fish knife, and soup spoon. The bread-and-butter plate with butter knife is placed at the upper left of the place setting with the water goblet and wineglass at the upper right. The dessert fork and spoon are set above the place card at the top center of the place setting.

Q How should the table be set for a buffet?

A A simple buffet table begins with a stack of warmed plates on a trivet facing hot casseroles of meat and vegetables, followed by a salad bowl and buttered rolls. If the table would appear crowded with the addition of the tableware, glasses of wine, the napkins, and flatware may be placed on a nearby, separate table.

Q How should the table be set for an informal tea?

A A tea tray is set in symmetry, from lower left: dessert forks, a basin for tea leaves, teapot, milk, sugar, and sugar tongs. At the upper left are tea plates and napkins, teacups with spoons resting on the saucers, hot water, and a plate of lemon slices.

∞984∞

Q If the newlyweds' dining area is small, what steps can be taken to make the space seem larger?

A First, the couple should avoid the use of platters and serving bowls on the dining table and, instead, set up a side table to hold the serveware or make up each guest plate with food in the kitchen and bring them to the table once the guests are seated.

∞985∞

Q How should fine china be arranged in cupboards to prevent damage?

A Fine china should either be stored in plate racks placed on cabinet shelves or stacked with a piece of flannel between each dish. Teacups should be hung separately from tiny hooks or stacked no more than two high on a shelf with ample space between the stacks.

∞986∞

Q How should crystal be arranged in cupboards to prevent damage?

A There should be plenty of space on the shelf between stems, which are stood right-side-up to protect their delicate rims. Crowding can result in tiny cracks and chips.

∽987∽

Q How should silverware be stored when not in use?

A Both sterling silver and silverplate items should be placed in a silver chest or drawer lined with tarnish-proof flannel. Silverware should not be wrapped in paper or plastic.

Couples should also avoid mixing silver items with stainless steel items in either the dishwasher or in storage.

∽988∽

Q How should couples care for their cookware?

A Each manufacturer will provide a specific list of hints to prolong the life of their cookware. Some basic suggestions are to never use metal utensils with nonstick-coated pans; never place wood-handled pans in the oven or dishwasher, and never use abrasive scouring pads.

∞989∞

Q What is the best way to store cookware?

A A growing number of manufacturers have developed pot racks that can be mounted from the wall or ceiling to hold pans and lids.

∞990∞

Q What is the first step to be taken when furnishing a new home?

A Couples should envision the lifestyle they will enjoy together and how they plan to entertain family members and friends. They should determine if they prefer a formal entertaining style or a casual approach.

∞991∞

Q What factors affect the furnishing of a new home?

A Couples should envision the amount of space they will have, coupled with color and design schemes they admire. They should anticipate the need to relocate and how their lifestyle will change as their careers advance.

∽992∽

Q How should couples set up a decorating budget for their new home?

A Couples should determine how much they can spend at the beginning and then each year to attain their dream house. Naturally, they will start by acquiring the basic necessities, then additional items for comfort, and finally, choose decorative accessories to complete the look.

∽993∽

Q Is it better to purchase a broad range of inexpensive items for the home or make expensive, individual purchases?

A Inexpensive sofas, cabinets, mattresses, and box springs are not good investments. Each of these items should be highly durable, so it's advisable to make an investment in quality with better construction and materials.

∽994∽

Q What ritual objects are traditional in a Jewish home?

A mezuzah is affixed to the doorpost at the entrance of the home and may be found at the entrance to each interior room, containing a small scroll with two biblical passages from the Book of Deuteronomy. It is a visible sign to all who enter of the residents' Jewish identity and commitment.

Shabbat candlesticks are often presented to the bridal couple as a special gift from their parents or a close family member. In some families, these candlesticks are passed down from generation to generation.

995

Q In what room of the home do newlyweds say they spend the most time together?

A A survey conducted by **Elegant Bride** concluded that newlyweds spend the majority of their time in the living room. Here, they watch television and relax together as well as entertain family members and friends.

996

Q What steps should be taken to set up a couple's finances after the wedding?

A Developing money habits as a couple may be a rather tough adjustment for some newlyweds. The first step is to determine the goals the couple are striving to attain—a new house, a new car, etc.—and then decide the strategies to reach the goal.

The next step is to set up a balance sheet that accounts for the couple's income and expenses. By taking a realistic look at their financial obligations and cash flow, the couple can attempt to structure their saving and spending.

∞997∞

Q What is the best way for a couple to manage their money after the wedding?

A There are several choices for a couple to choose in managing their money. They may consider a joint banking account that allows each of them to contribute as well as withdraw funds, or keep personal accounts after dividing up the financial responsibilities.

∞998∞

Q At what point should newlyweds begin thinking about retirement plans?

A Though retirement may be one of the farthest things on the minds of most newlyweds, it's a good idea to begin thinking about ways to fund a retirement lifestyle. Most couples today recognize that their company's 401K plan and Social Security will not provide adequate funds to maintain their desired lifestyle after they complete working.

Q What are some of the factors that determine how much credit a couple can afford?

A Positive credit use includes only buying things that the newlyweds' income can afford.

1000

Q What are the warning signs that a couple may be overextended on their credit commitments?

A Trouble signs include not knowing the amount owed until a bill arrives, making only minimum payments on credit cards and revolving charge accounts, juggling bill payments each month, going over the credit limit on credit cards, and having little or no savings to handle financial emergencies.

Index

Note: Numbers are questions numbers, not page numbers.

A

Aisle ribbon, 774
Aisle runner, 746
Almonds, 854
Alstroemeria, 479
American Gem Society, 13
Amethyst, 19
Anemone, 480
Announcements. *See also*
  Newspaper announce-
  ments
  of engagement, 43-54
  of wedding, 402-406
Aquamarine, 20
Aster, 481
"At home" cards, 407-410
Aufruf, 766
Azalea, 482

B

Bakers, 893-897
Bed linens, 704-711, 715
Best man, 118-120
  place at ceremony, 748
Betrothal ritual, 1
Birthday cakes, 920
Black tie, 352
Boning, 187
Bouquet, 435-436

preserving, 478
tossing, 436, 877-878,
  880-881
Boutonniere, 464-474
Bracelets, 277-278
Breaking the glass, 767
Bridal gowns, 141-213
  African-American, 210-211
  alterations, 207
  cleaning, 248
  costs, 202-203
  fabrics, 188-201
  formality and, 208-209
  heirloom, 252
  packing, 248
  preservation of, 246-251
  second-time bride, 212-
    213
  shopping for, 204-207
  sizes, 205
  stains on, 247, 789
  styles, 148-180
Bridal party. *See* Wedding
  party
Bridal registry, 395, 638-
  727
  cookware, 684-699
  definition, 638-639
  electrical appliances,
    700
  establishing, 641-649
  informing guests of, 720
  kitchen gadgets, 701, 703

kitchen linens, 702
linens, 702, 704-716
retailers, 718-719
tableware, 650-682
Bridal showers. *See*
Showers
Bridal trains, 162, 181
Bride. *See also specific topics*
carrying bouquet, 435
during ceremony, 753-
754, 757-760
engagement gift to
fiancé, 61
giving away, 800
hosting own wedding,
54
tossing bouquet. *See*
Bouquet
Bridesmaids, 112-114,
124, 752, 755, 756, 915
financial responsibility
of, 94, 114
flowers for, 437
gowns for, 214-219
jewelry for, 283
junior, 125

C

Cake knife, 898
Cake table, 463
Cakes. *See* Wedding cakes
Calla, 483
Calligrapher, 396

Camellias, 484
Cameras
restricting use of, 617
single-use, 618
Candlelight wedding, 777
Car decorations, 139-140
Carnations, 485
Caterers, 814-116, 820-
821, 823-824
Child attendants, 126, 750
clothes for, 221-222
China, 653-659, 985
Christian services, 358,
741
Chrysanthemums, 486
Chuppah, 764
Churches. *See* Houses of
worship
Civil ceremonies, 73, 732,
771-772
Clergy persons, 747
Clothes. *See specific items*
Coat check, 856
Coat of arms, 326
Confetti, 477. *See also* Rice
throwing
Conflicts, 82
Cookware, 684-699, 988-
989
knives, 697-699
materials, 685-690
types, 691-696
Corsages, 458
Couture bridal gown, 141
Cruises, 953-956
Crystal, 664-669, 986

D

Daffodils, 487
Daisies, 488, 492
Dancing, 555, 558, 559, 560-563, 873-875
Delphinium, 489
Diamonds, 9, 264
  carat, 36
  clarity of, 32
  color of, 31
  criteria for purchase, 30
  cut of, 33-35
  significance of, 21
  size, 36
Disc jockey, 560-563
Divorced parents of couple
  wedding photography and, 634
  wording for announcements, 53
  wording for invitations, 361-365
  wording for newspaper, 52
Double weddings, 360, 796-798
Duvets, 707-708

E

Earrings, 280-282
Electrical appliances, 700
Emerald, 22
Engagement
  announcement of, 43-54
  gifts, 60
  length of, 61
  parties, 55-59
  photos for, 584-587
  rings, 2-4, 7-42

F

Fashion. See specific items
Father-of-the-bride, 129-130, 757-760, 861
  asking for daughter in marriage, 1
  as deceased, 366, 758
  as divorced, 363, 365, 760
First home, 961-1000
  entertaining, 969-972
  finances, 996-1000
  ritual objects in Jewish home, 994
Florists, 424-426, 438, 784
Flower girl, 127
  dress for, 220
Flowers, 423-512. See also specific types
  boutonniere, 464-474
  choosing, 441-447

coordination, 431, 433
floral accents, 475
guest favors, 476
historical traditions, 428
language of, 423
price of, 440
ribbons, 432
as symbolism, 429-430, 456
Fondant, 906
Freesia, 490
Furniture, 990-992

G

Ganache, 905
Gardenia, 491
Garnet, 18
Garter toss, 876, 879, 880-881
Gemstones, 9, 17-30. *See also specific stones*
appraisals, 40
cut of, 33-35
Gerbera daisy, 492
Gift table, 882
Gifts. *See also* Bridal registry
acknowledgement cards, 419-420
for attendants, 135-138
engagement, 60
opening, 883

problems with, 725-727
Ginger, 493
Gladiolus, 494
Gloves, 284-295, 864
buttons, 286-290
color, 292
fabrics, 291
lengths, 284-285
rings and, 294
Gold, 15-16
Grandparents, 133, 243, 780
Groom
clothes for, 228-241, 244
giving ring, 2
hosting own wedding, 54
proposing, 3
taking his place at wedding, 748
Groom's cake, 911-914
Groomsmen, 121, 123-124, 755, 756
clothes for, 228-242
financial responsibility, 94
Guest lists
children on, 381
engagement parties, 59
reception, 78, 738-739
spouses of friends, 320
wedding, 78, 316-317, 319, 738-739
Guest registry, 786-787,

865
Guests
  accommodations, 91,
    386, 775-776
  after ceremony, 789
  children, 785
  dismissing from cere-
    mony, 782
  dress for male guests,
    245
  favors for, 89, 476, 853
  introducing, 788
  seating, 741-742
  travel information for,
    386
  welcoming, 740

packages, 930-931, 934
passports and visas,
  948-951
planning, 921-931
tipping, 932-934, 956
transportation, 934,
  936, 938-945, 952
Hosiery, 257-260
Houses of worship
  fees for, 731
  flowers for, 445-446,
    448-451
  photos in, 616
  with two aisles, 794
Hyacinthus, 495

H

Handbags, 296-297
Handkerchiefs, 298
Headpieces, 182-185, 261
Heirlooms, 252
Holloware, 973
Home. See First home
Honeymoon, 921-960
  cruises, 953-956
  financial considera-
    tions, 921, 925, 932-
    934, 937, 947, 953
  hotels, 933
  meals, 932, 935, 936
  origins of, 960

I

Insurance
  for rings, 42
Invitations. See also
  Stationery
  addressing, 308, 321,
    378-383
  direction card, 394
  dividing between fami-
    lies, 319
  enclosures, 376, 398
  engraved, 332
  envelopes, 377-380,
    398-400
  handwritten, 305, 396
  ink for, 333

issued by bride and
  groom, 370-372
mailing, 310-311
ordering, 307, 318
payment for, 309
pew card, 393
previewing, 306
reception, 322, 885
response cards, 388-392
RSVP, 387
for second wedding,
  373-374
selecting, 304, 314-315
sizes of, 328
thermographed, 332
tissue with, 397
titles on, 340-346, 375
tradition and, 303
wording, 334-375
Iris, 496

J

Jewelry. *See also specific types*
  for the bride, 262-282
  for bridesmaids, 283
Jewelry stores, 12-13
  customer service, 41
Jewish wedding ceremo-
  ny, 356-357, 742, 763-
  767. *See also* Houses of
  worship
"Jumping the broom," 762

K

Ketubah, 765
Kitchen gadgets, 701, 703
Kitchen linens, 702
Knives, 697-699

L

Letter sheet, 329-330
Lily, 497
Lily of the valley, 498
Linens, 702, 704-716
Lisianthus, 499

M

Magnolia, 500
Maid-of-honor, 115-117
Marriage
  in foreign countries,
    109, 959
  legal requirements,
    107-110, 959
Marriage ceremony, 728-
  802. *See also specific customs*; Wedding plans
  church bells, 802
  giving away bride, 800

interfaith, 761
involving friends, 734
kiss, 801
length of service, 737
order of service, 736, 743-753
personalizing, 733-734
symbols in, 762, 764-767, 769, 800-802
transportation issues, 735
Marriage licenses, 107-110
Matron-of-honor, 115-117
Menu cards, 850, 853
Military weddings, 359, 799
Mother-of-the-bride, 132, 779
clothes for, 224-227
as divorced, 362, 364
flowers for, 434, 458
seating, 746
as widow, 367-368
Mother-of-the-groom, 131, 779
clothes for, 224-227
flowers for, 434, 458
Music, 513-567
popular choices, 537-538
prelude, 743-744
selecting for reception, 542-548
selecting for wedding, 513-517, 534-438
types, 518-527, 554
Musicians, 529-533, 564-567
contracts for, 564
dress code, 530, 567
finances of hiring, 539-541, 564-566

N

Necklaces, 270-276
Newspaper announce-ments, 47-54
costs, 49
information in, 48
photographs, 49
Nuptial Mass, 358

O

Opal, 27
Orchid, 501
Outdoor wedding, 772-778

P

Pansy, 502

Parents of bride
  as deceased, 366, 370, 780
  divorced, 52-53, 361-
    365, 634
  expenses, 90
  invitations and, 354
  meeting parents of
    groom, 62
Parents of groom
  expenses, 92
  invitations and, 355
  meeting parents of
    bride, 62
Parking, 776
Passports and visas, 948-
  951
Pearl, 23, 265-271
Peony, 503
Pets, 81
Pew card, 393
Photo journalism, 592
Photographers/Videograp
    hers, 783
  booking, 576, 610
  confirming, 577
  dress code, 608
  financial matters, 578-
    582, 611, 637
  meetings with, 583,
    588, 589
  number of, 627
  presentations, 572
  role in wedding, 589,
    590, 612, 622-623, 629,
    636

selecting, 568-572, 609
Photography, 568-637
  for engagement, 584-
    587
  film, 573
  hand-colored, 575
  for newspaper, 49
  occasions needing, 635
  with pets, 81
  posed versus candid
    shots, 588, 591
  preparing for getting
    picture taken, 601-603,
    614, 615
  proofs, 593
  sepia-toning, 574
  wedding album, 594-
    597, 605-606, 619-620
  wedding portrait, 598-
    604
Pineapple, 504
Place cards, 849, 853
Platinum, 15
Pomander, 457
Processional, 745
Proposals, 3

Q

Queen Anne's lace, 505

R

Receiving lines, 795, 857-866
Reception card, 352-353, 384-385
Receptions, 803-886
  after honeymoon, 79-80
  cash bar, 827
  cocktail hour, 826-828
  dancing, 555, 558, 559, 560-563, 873-875
  favors, 89, 476, 853
  financial matters, 804, 823-825
  flowers for, 451-455, 459-461, 848
  formality of, 811-813
  locations of, 803, 805, 807-809, 884
  menu for, 810, 814-819, 826, 829-833
  music for, 542-563
  tables, 463, 844-855
Recessional, 781
Rehearsals, 770, 791-793
Relationships, 962-968
Response cards, 388-392
Rice throwing, 789-790
Ring bearer, 128, 751
  clothes for, 223
Rings
  alternatives, 10
  appraisals, 40
  in ceremony, 751
  customer services for, 41
  diamond, 9, 21, 30-37
  engagement, 2-4, 7-38, 68
  gemstones, 9, 17-30
  gimmal, 6
  groom's wedding band, 38
  insurance, 42
  payment of, 7, 38-39
  settings, 15-17
  when worn, 68
  where worn, 8
  while wearing gloves, 294
Rose, 506
Ruby, 24

S

Sapphire, 26
Sardonyx, 25
Save-the-date cards, 312-313
Shoes, 253-256
Showers, 721-724
  hosting, 95
Silver, 15
Silver flatware, 670-681, 987
Statice, 507
Stationery, 324-327
  calligrapher, 396
  monogram, 416
  for thank-you notes, 415
Stephanotis, 508

Sunflower, 510

T

Table linens, 716
Table setting, 979-983
Tableware, 650-682, 974-987
Tasting, 822
Thank-you notes, 411-420
Threshold, 961
Titles on invitations, 340-346, 375
Toasts
    at engagement parties, 57-58
    wedding, 867-872
Topaz, 28
Towels, 712-714
Travel agents, 927-931, 938
Tulip, 511
Tuquoise, 29

U

Undergarments, 299-302
Underlining, 186
Unity candle, 769
Ushers, 122-123, 740, 746

V

Veils, 183-184
Videos, 568-637. *See also*
    Photographers/Videographers; Photography
    copyrighted music, 631
    dubbing, 632
    financial considerations, 623, 633
    length of, 628
    pacing, 625
    popularity of, 607
    prewedding, 626
    video interviews, 630

W

Waiters, 820
Watermark, 325
Wedding album, 594-597, 605-606. *See also*
    Photography
    table shots, 619-620
Wedding cakes, 887-920
    bridesmaids charms and, 915
    dietary restrictions and, 892
    flavors, 907-908
    flowers for, 462-463
    fondant, 906
    ganache, 905
    ordering, 900
    prices, 891, 899, 901
    serving, 834-842, 902-903, 916-917

top layer, 918-919
Wedding director, 134
Wedding fashion. *See specific items*
Wedding party, 115-117, 214-219
  signing guest registry, 787
  taking their place at ceremony, 747-753
Wedding plans
  budgets, 83-85, 87-88, 90-94, 731-732
  civil ceremonies, 73, 732, 771-772
  conflicts, 82
  facilities of wedding, 730
  initial discussions, 63-64
  location of wedding, 729, 772-773, 775-777
  organizing, 96, 728-736
  prioritizing, 86
  professional coordinators, 97-101
  rehearsals, 770
  setting date, 69-73
  time for, 67
Wedding portrait, 598-604. *See also* Photography
Wedding program, 401, 768

Wedding rhymes, 142
Wedding weekend, 102-105
Weddings. *See also* Receptions; *specific topics*
  cancellation, 422
  ceremony. *See* Marriage ceremony
  finishing touches, 89
  on holidays, 439, 527
  at home of friends, 369
  location, 77
  out-of-town, 106
  postponements, 421
  style of, 64-66
  time of day, 75-76
White tie, 353
Wristwatches, 279

Z

Zinnia, 512